I0169213

the big-boobed bridesmaid
by Sybil Priebe

Copyright © 2014 Sybil Priebe.
All rights reserved.

ISBN: 0989194418
ISBN-13: 978-0-9891944-1-9

BBB

This book is dedicated to
all the sexy goofballs* in my life who are
smart, hilarious, & independent – the trifecta.

*Especially KJ.

BBB

Chapter 1: The Short Introduction...6
Chapter 1.5: The Long Introduction. 8
Chapter 2: The First Memories. 11
Chapter 3: And The Weddings...13
Chapter 4: In The Beginning = December 2012. 16
Sideboob #1: More Pictures. 17
Chapter 5: January 2013...20
Chapter 6: February 2013...26
Sideboob #2: If I Pass Away...41
Chapter 7: March 2013. (Month One.)...42
Sideboob #3: Follow-Up Questions...68
Chapter 8: Mid-March 2013, Back to School. 69
Sideboob #4: Contradictory..94
Chapter 9: April 2013. (One Month Post-Op.)..95
Sideboob #3:...116
Chapter 10: May 2013. (Two Months Post-Op.)......................................121
Chapter 11: June 2013 (Three Months Post-Op).....................................130
Chapter 12: July 2013 (Four Months Post-Op). 144
Sideboob #5: Maid of the Mono-Boob...151
Chapter 13: August 2013 (Five Months Post-Op).....................................152
Chapter 14: September 2013 (Six Months Post-Op)..................................161
Chapter 15: October 2013 (Seven Months Post-Op)..................................173
Chapter 16: November 2013 (Eight Months Post-Op).................................179
Chapter 17: December 2013 (Nine Months Post-Op). 186
Chapter 18: January 2014 (Ten Months Post-Op)......................................188
Chapter 19: February 2014 (Eleven Months Post-Op.)................................196
Chapter 20: March 2014 (One Year Post-Op)..201
Chapter 21: April 2014..208
Chapter 22: May 2014...220
Chapter 23: June 2014...226
Chapter 24: Conclusion. 235
References. 236
Attributions..237
Appendix (Chapter 25)..238
About the Author..240

BBB

Chapter 1: The Short Introduction.

Hi there.
My eyes are up here.
Hee hee hee. Just a little boob humor for ya.

Let's start with just a little bit about me:
My name is Sybil. I grew up in North Dakota, and pretty much never left even to attend college. Currently, I'm in the middle of my ninth year of teaching college composition & humanities courses at a fun, rural community college; I've taught for over fifteen years total (started out at the high school level, etc.).

I'm living with my boyfriend and bitchy cat in a house we bought in the summer of 2011. He & I have been together for over ten years at this point, and he officially moved into our home on a permanent basis the day after my surgery... but more on that later...

This book and its contents revolve around my breast reduction surgery. I say "revolve" because for me, this surgery was about more than just chopping off two pounds of fat from my chest. This surgery was about body issues for me, and then it lead into other concerns and ideas and situations (like weight loss).

(Please note that this surgery did not occur because I had or have breast cancer.)

When I got home from my surgery, I remember resting in bed, in our remodeled master bedroom, with my iPad on my lap. I was browsing Amazon.com for a book or story about someone who had gone through breast reduction surgery. "Who had been on my journey before?" I wondered. I couldn't find anything that wasn't related to breast cancer. I did find blogs – some scary ones at that! – and I thought, "Oh hell! I'll write down my journey then, since I'm a writer (and teacher of writing), and that way others might be able to benefit from it." Just because I had nothing to reference doesn't mean others should have to go through this blindly either.

So, I went back to my private blog that keeps track of my thoughts about many things and found excerpts that pertains to this particular event (the lead-up, etc.). I've added some pre-surgery thoughts and stories, but mostly, this book is concentrated on the recovery part – all the way to one year after the surgery!

+And while I pride myself in my writing skills, this book embraces wabi sabi= meaning, it is imperfect. But, that's okay with me.

Chapter 1.5: The Long Introduction.

I had never liked my large chest. Never, never, never, never. And I'm not going to bash those women who love theirs. Good for you, I say. (Pat yourselves on your... chesticles?)

But for myself, I didn't like them for many reasons.

One of the mental reasons I never felt connected to my breasts was that my large chest connected me to my mother. She's got a large set on her, and none of my sisters do, so, yes, I had "inherited" those genes. I haven't always gotten along with my mom, so that didn't help the situation. She also never seemed hindered by her chest; she still participated in intramural volleyball and golf. I never heard her complain about back pain, either. So, in turn, I was supposed to just deal with my large breasts because she had. This was made apparent to me when I first brought up a breast-reduction years ago; my dad said, "You aren't that large." And he was probably comparing me to her, because comparing me to my sister would've yielded a different response.

Another mental reason was that when I would see large breasts on other women, I often thought they looked sloppy and not "put-together." It seems like the larger a woman is on top, the more likely it is that she won't be wearing the right bra and they will be all over the place. "Oh, I'm not THAT size," a woman will say because, you know, wearing a larger cup size means she's... a stripper? (I was told that by a customer service rep once upon a time; I was trying to order a size 34G bra.)

I want to look put-together, of course. And I do sometimes feel they looked over-sexualized. Whether a woman "uses" her chest for attention or not (and I was told by many I should've used mine for persuasion!), she is seen as less intelligent and more sexual. I wanted no part of that. I still don't. I value my intelligence too much. Now, some would say that using one's chest for manipulation is smart, and I suppose they might be partly right. I just don't want anything to do with that kind of persuasion. Period.

The physical reasons were plentiful. The athletics I wanted to participate in. The back aches. The search for bras. The wish to go swimming without a neck ache or the task of keeping "it all" tucked away inside the god damn bikini top.

I was an athletic kid. My mom threw me into her favorite sport – volleyball – early on. I liked it for awhile. I wasn't a great setter, and I wasn't as quick as others. There was a girl who went to the all the off-season camps; she was a better setter than I, even if she was large-chested. I noticed this. She was larger than I was, yet could move. "Good for her," I thought. I didn't care to be good in order for the coach and my mom to appreciate me more. I rarely fell for peer pressure from anyone, and that may have been the seed that created many issues for me – when you don't feel pressured to do things, you end up with too many options (and some say more options lead to more stress).

Later, I recall seeing photos of my mother playing intramural volleyball – her chest smooched between her arms as she bumped the ball. It looked uncomfortable.

Instead of volleyball, I fell for tennis. My freshman year of high school was when I started that sport, and I loved it and the coach. I didn't like, of course, how my chest kept me from being quick on my feet. I remember saying to a boyfriend at the time that I wished I could velcroe the breasts I had on and off. On for him, and off for tennis. I was convinced I'd be faster and happier without them. Hell, he could have them on my down time and play with them – velcroe them to his own chest for all I care. I was not attached to them like I was attached to my hair.

Big breasts, big hair. Isn't that how it is in Texas?

There was a largeness I felt overall just because of them. This came to my attention with my college boyfriend, who pointed out as we were going to bed that my small waist was hiding behind my drooping chest.

I don't remember being a B. I think I was a C immediately... Luckily, my high school years hit during the grunge "era," and I was able to cover them up. In a beer garden later on in college, high school classmates would ask me if my breasts were fake because they'd "never noticed them before." I knew that the large tees and pants during those high school years kept me well-hidden. And since people rarely came to our tennis games, no one noticed my actual body size.

So... this book is for those who have had non-cancerous-based issues with their breasts for whatever reason. Maybe they got implants for a husband and detest them or they were "that girl" who matured way too quickly or they just simply saw themselves happier in a different body – one they couldn't create with diet & exercise. Notes:

As I was copying and pasting my journal entries, I did edit out any "drama" that wasn't directly related to the surgery, so that's where one might see the brackets and ellipses being used: [...]. Also, I did spellcheck and add in words to make the sentences more clear. Most people know that journaling is sometimes only clear to the journaler – so I had to clarify things for you all. Duh!

Also, when you see "Part 2" or "Part 3" after a date, that means it was later on in the day. I didn't want to bother with time stamps.

Lastly, I tried to be consistent with my numbers (spelling out those under 10, blahblahblah). I'm guessing only other English teachers will notice the glitches in this?

Chapter 2: The First Memories.

My first two memories that have anything to do with my chest or weight are etched in my brain.

The first one.

I am a preteen who is about 10 or 11-years-old, and my breasts are just starting to make their way out of my body. They are very small and contain "rocks" as I like to call them. I've noticed this change, and it's not sitting with me very well. I don't think I wanted to change, but what kid does?

We're at my uncle's lake cabin on a summer day. I'm wearing a pale yellow pocket tee. As I head out onto the deck of the cabin, which leads to the beach, my uncle is with other people to my left. He's sitting at the picnic table. Perhaps he's had a drink or two, or perhaps not. I shut the screen door behind me, and he says, "Hey, Sybil, are you growing boobs or is there something in your pocket?"

Immediately, I'm ashamed of what's happening to my stupid body. Others can see things changing on me, and it pisses me off. I should've been more upset with my uncle at the time, but I was too ashamed of not being able to hide my body from his perverted view.

The second one.

I'm about the same age as the first memory, and we're in the living room. I say "we're" because I'm sitting on the couch with my mom and sisters. Alisa is three years younger than I am, and we are built the same – athletic. Our sister Robin is and always has been lanky and slim. She is six years younger than I am.

Our mom says something in the middle of a conversation we're having. She says something like, "You two [meaning Alisa & I] know you will never have bodies like Robin, right?"

Now, maybe it was a slip-up on her part. Maybe she had been compared to her sisters for all of time. Maybe she didn't like the body she was in, but I still don't think that was something a mom should say to her daughters. She insinuated that we'd be larger, and that that was bad and that we should brace ourselves for dealing with it. And it was obviously something she should not have said because it has been stuck in my head for over twenty years now.

Chapter 3: And The Weddings.

Summer 2005:

I'm out in Portland, Oregon for Fran's wedding. She's one of my best friends, and she's small on top, so of course she assigns us bridesmaids strapless gowns. The other two bridesmaids – her sister and her good friend Bevie – are also smaller on top than I am. Much smaller. Needless to say, I was popping out of the dress and very uncomfortable.

Spring/Summer 2008:

My brother Jed and his girlfriend Hilary get engaged, and she doesn't ask me to be a bridesmaid. My brother, instead, asks me to be his attendant. I was relieved and excited that I would choose my own dress. It was black with straps large enough to hide my minimizer bra. Amen.

I'm actually not trying to show my cleavage in this shot; I had to bend over a bit in order to fit my melon in the iMac's Photobooth screen. So, yeah, the cleavage was not noticeable unless a person was towering above me.

Summer 2009:

My sister Robin is engaged to Nick, and we all go bridesmaid shopping. Even Nick comes with. We're all trying on various styles, and up to this point, no one agrees with me that we should bypass strapless gowns. Because EVERYONE is smaller than I am in the boobage department. So, I grab a strapless gown in my size, stomp into a fitting room, and chuck the minimizer bra off and the dumb dress on. When I come out, immediately I have my future brother-in-law on my side.

His eyes say it all.

They say, "Oh, god no. That is a sea of boobs that we don't need."

My brain concurs with a "DUH."

Thankfully, Robin was in favor of a tea-length dress that had straps and pockets. The straps were not quite wide enough to cover a minimizer, so I wore an unsupportive white bra that is seen in many of their wedding pictures because I guess I can't not dance like a psycho.

Chapter 4: In The Beginning = December 2012.

I had a conversation with my sister Alisa over Christmas Break about doing the Half Marathon again (in Fargo in May), but in the middle of thinking about doing it, I realized I didn't want to train with THIS chest again. I knew my legs could handle another round of training like they did a few years ago (May 2011 was my first Half Marathon), but I didn't want to try to tie down the goddamn boobs again. Just thinking about all that – the stress of finding 2-3 bras to put on every morning & the hassle – took all the possible fun out of the idea of training again.

Then, on New Year's Eve, I meet one of my sister's friends who has had the surgery. She's been on a rampage to lose weight, and her surgery was the catalyst for that loss. The friend tells me, as every woman who I talk to about this surgery says, that she doesn't regret the decision. This conversation makes the decision in my head turn from cement to concrete.

Sideboob #1: More Pictures.

This first set will make ya'll think, "She wasn't big!" But just hold your bras, okay.

<u>Above</u>: Me filming the Homecoming Parade 2009; me at my cousin's wedding in Duluth, MN in the summer of 2010; my boyfriend's Christmas Party in 2011.

These pictures above could be in a "How-To" Guide for hiding large chests.
First of all, wear minimizers.
Use scarves if it's cold enough out.
Wear black cardigans with things.
When you take a picture, hunch forward.
Try wearing V-necked shirts (see below); sometimes, it works.

<u>Below</u>: What I was dealing with, for real. The first row is from the summer of 2006. Yes, the middle photo is a picture of my boyfriend and I at a wedding.

Summer 2009

Summer 2010

Summer 2012

<u>Bottom Row</u>: You can see that I tried the black cardigan idea for the summer 2009 picture, and the top I'm wearing for the summer 2012 photo was roomy. (As I went through my recovery, and tried to find good pictures of a "Before," it was difficult.)

Now, some might say, "Well, you look hourglass-shaped; it's fine!" or whatever else. But here's thing, I don't really care what others perceived about what I was going through. They weren't in my body, and, therefore, had no say. I mean, would you tell someone who is walking "just fine" that they don't need a knee replacement? Or a person who lifts large objects constantly (um, Dad!) that they don't need back surgery? What I heard when people said those things was, "Just deal with it." And I just didn't want to. I also didn't think I had to just to make everyone else happy either. Plus, what was my surgery going to do TO THEM anyhow? It wasn't like I was going to have a facelift, and they'd end up with a sister/cousin/daughter/friend who looked strange to everyone!

Chapter 5: January 2013.

So, I found the courage to ask my regular doctor, at my annual visit, about the idea of reduction. We chatted, and she listened. She had no clue how large I was (bra-size-wise), yet was very helpful. I think she has seen me out and about, being active by running and biking and walking (because I have seen her). Speaking of being active, I know she has lost weight, too. I've never asked her about it, but she went from probably over 200lbs herself to much less than that in a year. I recall coming in for my annual a year or two ago, and thinking for a split second that I had the wrong doctor.

Perhaps, underneath her concerned smile was someone who had had the same weight issues in her head.

Anyhow, she said she'd put a call into the Plastic Surgery "department" up at Sanford in Fargo. She asked if I wanted a female surgeon, and I said yes.

Tomorrow is my plastic surgery consultation. I didn't tell my boss details about it.

I'm worried that the doc won't be able to do it over Spring Break. I'm worried it could potentially not get covered under insurance. I'm mostly worried about the former than the later; they are HUGE. Anyhow... I really hope she can cut me open March 8 or 9 or 10 or 11 or 12... hopefully, she doesn't do vacations when college students do. Yeah.

Facebook Conversation:

KJ:
In honor of a missed safety meeting today... I am drinking a glass of wine at home, while my boys drink their juice boxes. I made a plate of chips-n-cheese, because I wanted an appetizer. Wine is fairly decent, one I made myself from a kit! However, the conversation seems to be lacking. What could be missing? Well, Sybil and Cheryl, of course.

Cheryl:
Meetings... Sodamfun!

Me:
We chatted briefly in Cheryl & Bill's office about having a Bye Bye Boobies party for me in mid-Feb!

KJ:
Great theme for a party!

Cheryl:
Bill calls it a memorial service!

KJ:
That is funny. Definitely funny.

Me:
I think I'll wear something low-cut and slutty; people could take some last pics with "the big girls" before they become smaller girls.

Cheryl:
It will be many of our first glance at the bodacious cleavage!!

Me:
True. Jan's definitely hoping I show off the smaller ladies more.

January 16, 2013:

I had to fill out a sheet of questions yesterday at the Plastic Surgery office. Do you have back pain? Do you find it difficult to fit into shit? Do you take drugs for your back pain? Are you sick of having large boobies?

Yes to all, man. It was kind of shocking. I mean, I know my chest is large, but when every freaking answer in my head was "yes," I knew that this "my boobs are too big" idea wasn't just in my head.

So, the surgeon measures me. My left breast is wider but perkier than rightie. She uses some chart and then declares that she'll be able to take over 600 grams from each breast. Since Blue Cross/Blue Shield only requires a woman to take out 200 for it to be covered, the surgeon was positive they'd approve it. I was relieved, and yet shocked that I had THAT MUCH extra poundage. Good lord.

The little, sweet nurse Erica took some "Before" pictures and then I was on my merry way.

Needless to say, and to keep this short, re-reading the <u>Why Men Love Bitches</u> book has brought a refreshing attitude to my life. I'm worried more so about me and my shit and less about HIM AND ME AND US. It's awesome. I've ignored his calls and texts lately, and he's been semi-upset in a good way about it.

Plus, he's on board with my breast reduction surgery. He was turned on by it, actually, while we ate lunch at Red Lobster Tuesday. Well, he was actually eyeing my shirt because it had unbuttoned itself; I tell him at the restaurant (or later?) that after this surgery, I'll probably "show them off more" because I will LIKE them.

He has had his own "life-changing" events happen to him. He wants to leave his workplace for good and move down to Wahpeton & our house officially. He doesn't want to commute anymore or live in Fargo half-time anymore. It was THAT kind of weekend for him = one massive eye-opener!

So, all is well. Yeah. Better than well, I suppose. And I'm pooped out.

Oh, and it looks like surgery will be March 1... my dept chair was cool about it, and I simply said I had a non-life-threatening surgery to take care of. I don't think he can legally ask me much more. I guess it could be noticeable, but whatever. Many people on campus take vacays and shit like that (or have babies and surgeries). Plus, I typically go to a conference for a whole week in the spring (Writer's conference at UND). When my guilt pops up over this, I'll think of the things I just mentioned. AND I'll think of how my students don't want to show up that week before break anyhow.

Looking through the images online (on Pinterest.com mainly), I see a lot about forgiveness. And eventually, or in the near future, I need to forgive mom for her body image issues. She shows off her chest, yet I wasn't allowed to in that one Christmas outfit (brown velvet with a keyhole at the chest).

She's got similar issues now with my breast reduction surgery; she mentioned, after I gave her and my dad the news about this upcoming surgery, that my stomach now would look larger (or something to that effect). This time around, I see her own issues pop through. I see that she's got the issues & I don't... I see her for all the inner work she hasn't done in order to like herself. It's sad, really. Do kids sometimes feel wiser than their parents, at some point?

Huh.

I'm excited for less chest. Excited for less back pain & aches. I'm excited for less insecurity over these things on me that I don't feel affection for. I know god wants me to appreciate them, and I tried, but George Carlin (one of my idols – no joke!) would say to make one's self feel better* is a grand idea. People change their bodies permanently all the time = surgery is everywhere! Knee replacements & back pain relief, to name things my parents have done.

*If I feel better about me, it'll probably lead to a domino effect. Happy for others, content with change, grateful for all I have, etc.

"That's money, honey."

My boyfriend just had a few thousand dollars stolen from him.

So, I guess it makes me grateful for my life. And, unfortunately or fortunately, he may have to work longer at the bar. His dream of moving down here in March full-time might not work. His self-worth is so tied to money, yet he spends it more now than when I was first with him. We've switched roles, oddly enough; I'm the saver now.

Anyhow, I told him it's just money.

January 24, 2013:

So, I guess it's my birthday tomorrow.

Yeah. I'll be 36 in a few hours. And I only really feel old because I'm not super healthy. Just think, when I turn 37, I should be smaller on top at least and that's awesome.

I'm going to try to get some awesome sleep, teach two classes as fun as I can, grade/assess some shit to get semi-caught up, and then bake myself my own damn cake just in case my dad, who is sick, didn't. Last year, they bought me a cookie cake. No no no. Those are not my cup of tea.

Okay. Bye 35. You were fun times.

This last year taught me a lot about... about having fun & traveling with my boyfriend to NYC, about publishing, about my strength in rough times on campus, about being a good aunt & teacher to Audrey, about having the kitchen I love... 35 saw Gpa die, but that's okay because he's not in pain anymore and he left a lot of good people behind.

Here's to 36!

January 31, 2013:

Mammogram Day. Luckily, Blue Cross/Blue Shield of North Dakota covers one mammogram from the ages of 35-39, so this was one less payment for me to worry about.

It was highly uncomfortable, but the little teeny pregnant Radiologist was sweet about it all.

Afterwards, Jan and I went to Best Buy to look at TVs. There were a lot of Super Bowl specials, and we eyed the 50" Samsung. We had been discussing moving the 42" that is in the living room up to the master bedroom for my recovery. Before we leave Best Buy to have dinner with my family at the Mexican Village, we see that a 55" one is on sale for $50 more than the 50" one we originally thought we'd buy.

At dinner, no one asks how my mammogram went. No one. My siblings all chat, instead, about upcoming trips to warmer temps. This really bugs Jan; he wants everyone to be more concerned, but part of me thinks they are just focused on their own lives – or perhaps they don't know how to ask me about it?

After dinner, we stop back at Best Buy to purchase the big TV. And an entertainment center for it to sit on, too.

Chapter 6: February 2013.

There is this need in me to publish. And I'm working on this textbook. It's so me, it's ridiculous. And I want to write more and more after. Forever. I don't care if no one reads it. I don't care if 500 people think it sucks if 250 cool people think it's awesome sauce.

I will always be a work-in-progress. I'm okay with that; I actually like that label. True story.

A private Facebook message I sent to a close friend:

So, everyone else who is close to me know this, so you should too.

I'm having breast reduction surgery on March 1. Over holiday break, Alisa & I were talking about running the Half Marathon in May, and I was like, "Ugh, these damn boobs!" Like, they are what keep me from being more active (I tend to be lazy, in general, but three sports bras ain't fun)... so yeah.

Last summer, I ran into a girl from high school who said she got hers covered by insurance. And, I realized between talking to Alisa (and her friends on New Year's Eve who've had it done) & my doctor, that I have wanted a smaller chest forever. My back aches everyday, and I'm sick of just dealing with it.

SO at my annual appt in January, I asked my doc about it. She referred me, I've had a few consultations & a mammogram (to check for cancer), and yeah... here's to 34C/Ds in less than a month! Goodbye 34G/H! I'm mostly excited, but a little freaked out about the possible pain after - some say they felt fine in a few days, etc. My surgeon insisted on two weeks of doing nothing. I'm using sick leave for the week before Spring Break, and then I should be ready to rock after... I can't run or exercise heavily for a month after, but I could probably do the 5K in May (if I felt up to it, etc.) and maybe try for the Half in October.

At first Jan wasn't on board. But after my consultation, and him realizing she could take two pounds of strain (yes, Blue Cross/Blue Shield requires 200g to be reduced, and I have 600+g in each! Jeezus), he was like, "Will you show them off more? Will you have more self-confidence?"

Speaking of him, he's quitting at the Turf; his last day will probably be Feb. 28 so he can take care of me for the first few days after my surgery. We even bought a new TV for the living room, so I can have one upstairs while I heal.

Okay, this has been the longest message in the world.

LOVE & Miss you! I may invite your sister [who lives in town] to my "Bye Bye Boobies" party.

February 10, 2013 (Part 2):

Another Facebook conversation:

Me:
To add to your question from last night... My surgery is on a Friday & I'm using sick leave for the week between that & Spring Break. Some women have said they didn't need two weeks to recover, but my surgeon was firm about it.

I've only told my dept chair that I'm having a "non-life-threatening" surgery; I don't know if he'll understand why I NEED this reduction - guys don't always get it. [...] It might be noticeable after, but I've only told people I trust thus far.

It was awesome to see you last night!!!

Bethany:
It was fun last night! And I would want to keep my chest info on the DL too... so don't worry... I won't say a word! Excited for you... let me know if I can help in anyway! I'll be thinking of you!

Me:
The weird thing is, I knew I could trust Jane right away! I wish I felt that way about more people!
Thanks for letting me ask what size you are; that was a lil' blunt on my part, but I have no frame of reference.

I'm excited, too. Thanks, hun!

Bethany:
Haha...I'm blunt 99% of the time...I get it!

February 12, 2013:

Diet Coke.
I almost mistyped the subject above and put "Diet Cock." Who'd want that kind of diet? Or that kind of cock? Jeezus Pete.

Okay, so I was just thinking, in the middle of assessing my ASSsssssss off, that I wish I could look at food like I do Diet Coke. I rarely drink that crap anymore. And I'm okay with how far back I have cut myself off from it. I don't crave it or anything. And for awhile there, back in November, I barely wanted sugar (dessert) after meals. I didn't feel that pull for something sweet when I was eating better & less. Ugh.

I am just not consistent. I lose a few pounds (didn't I lose like 6-10 within a few weeks by cutting back a little bit and lowering my sugar intake?) and then I have a few days of pure crap and lose that edge to eat less.

So, I need to work on consistency. Maybe I should keep track of each day that I "do right" by myself & my stomach. If I can do like seven in a row, I should reward myself. Or, hell, 30 in a row! I mean, christ! I'll be 200 pounds forever at this rate, and I recall telling myself never to get to this point again after I did in grad school. I was wearing 18s then, but barely fitting into 16s at the Gap right now ain't any better.

I hope chopping my boobs down will add to this need to slim down. And I hope I get back into running. I miss it. It was such a stress reliever. A big one, for sure.

Plus, everyone around here has big boobs. I, sadly, equate them (unless they are fake), with laziness. Because I know how much my activity decreases with having to haul them around.

Today, I had a bowl of cereal (the high protein kind = Great Grains) & water with my vitamins & coffee later before lunch. At lunch with Megan, I had water & salad and 1/2 of the chicken enchilada. I don't forsee myself needing a snack later, but if so, I hope to make it a healthy-ish one (2 cups of popcorn)... followed by a protein-based dinner.

February 14, 2013:

Up to Fargo, again, for my last pre-op appointment. I ask whether the weather will come into play – it's been a shitty winter – and the surgeon says, "Honey, I live blocks away. I will be there!" This unimportant bit of information oddly calms my nerves.

Once again, Jan and I head to Best Buy for a TV wall mount. That's a romantic purchase on Valentine's Day, isn't it? ☺ Our true personalities shine through in times like that; I don't get buyer's remorse, so the minute I see a remotely good wall mount for a decent price, I'm sold and ready to head out. He likes to research and think about it. This is like my brother who has probably never purchased anything without writing – in his head – a research paper about it. Complete with cited sources and interviews.

February 16, 2013:

I thought it was an innocent trip to Walmart, but once I brought up how my younger siblings' quest for marriage and kids left me and my sister off the hook for guilt trips from my parents... he asked if I really thought I was never going to have kids.

This threw me for a loop.

So, we had the longest conversation about babies. He wants them &
sees them in our plan for this summer already (the trying part
anyway). I'm overwhelmed. VERY!

He made some good points yet was shocked that I didn't think I
wanted them. And I've honestly figured with him working in Fargo
and us not being married, it wasn't in the plan. I think a woman with
a biological clock would've asked him sooner about it all, right?

It's a sticky situation & one that comes after an awesome Valentine's
Day & weeks of us feeling okay & like the couple I imagined for us...
NOW things are not what I thought they'd be. People say: "It's never
a good time to have babies." I guess not. And this conversation
comes out of left field, for me. We've never really discussed it much.
Now, he says he's kind of coming down here to be with me AND
start a family.

The weight of a gorilla found its way to my mind. And shoulders.

February 16, 2013 (Part 2):

A Facebook conversation:

Me:
Hello close, sister-like, monkeys,
So, Jan & I had a huge discussion today about having kids. HUGE.
I'm exhausted & overwhelmed. For a long time, I didn't think it was
in the cards for us - him living/working in Fgo, etc. - but now with
him moving down here, he wants parenthood to be a part of our
future plans... like trying even this summer to have one after I'm
healed from my surgery.

I have been conflicted over this... a constant debate in my head. Half
wants kids; half is like "why?"...

I'm looking to my best buds for advice. You know me well & I know
you'll be honest.

big hug -Sybil

KJ:
I need some time to process. Huge is right! Positive I think but so
huge! You cannot just throw something like that just out there!

Me:
I need time to process too.

We've barely talked the rest of the day & I can't sleep. He's upset;
I'm upset... We just had an awesome Valentine's Day on Thursday,
too. Everything seems screwed up. Hopefully he & I can have a
better discussion soon. I need to think this kind of major decision
through!!

KJ:
Fortunately you have time. I think the stress and anxiety is justified.
Now take a deep breath and maybe turn off the logical part of your
mind. If possible have some fun exploring the topic with him
without the reality of all the compilations that kids bring. It might
help you see the fun side before contemplating the complex
situation.

Me:
Thanks, KJ... he mentioned in our heated conversation how "don't
you want a little you running around?" & he admitted he dislikes
going to Audrey's celebration-stuff because I dote on her ("Why
don't we have children you can dote on?")... the logical parts (the
physical toll & financial strain) would be all on me, for the most
part. I don't want to resent him.

Plus, maybe we should be married first? I don't know... I just got the
feeling this could've been approached differently from him. More "I
love you/want you to be the mother to my kids" instead of "I want
kids & thought you did too, so make up your mind about this."

So, I woke up around 1am, came downstairs to eat something (we
didn't have dinner) & he was watching TV, drinking more beer than
usual. I sat down for a minute & asked if he had been making noise
(heard a thump which woke me up); he said no & "should I be
quieter?" with a really angry look on his face. Ugh!

Once I got to sleep, I dreamt he had cheated on me over these ten
years with many girls. I broke up with him, in dramatic fashion...
Ugh; I hate those dreams.

Anyhow, it's just a sticky situation. He's moving here & doesn't have
a job lined up; I'm getting a surgery done I've wanted forever.

Blech. And I just feel so not me. Almost a bit depressed that I'm not 100% sure about all this kid stuff.

KJ:
Saying a prayer for a little peace and smiles.

Cheryl:
You've got a lot to process. I am with KJ, this is one that does need to be decided with an eye to the feelings side of it, not the logistics. You have a good job, even if he was Mr. Mom, you'd not have such a huge financial strain. I can't imagine you'd resent him, if he was doing his share of the work. An at-home parent is really nice, if you can swing it.

Cheryl:
As far as being married, I agree. Maybe you could talk again and let him know that part of your hesitation is wanting a permanent commitment before making babies. The two of you aren't big on talking about feelings, but I think you really do need to get that out on the table as part of this whole discussion.

I do remember a few years ago, you said you had realized you wanted to get married and have kids. But, then when Jan didn't seem to want that, you seemed to sort of accept it, and then settle on the status quo.
Be sure to explore why you don't think you want kids, if it's you, or it's that you had resigned yourself to it not being in the cards.

KJ is right, also, you do have time to explore this and make a decision without feeling rushed or pressured. But tell Jan what you're feeling about all of it. It is a new thing for you guys, the whole open feeling talk thing, but it can be rewarding!

Love you! I will be praying, too!

Me:
Thank you...

We decided in the middle of the convo yesterday that we shouldn't bring up the past because we were both assuming A LOT; he assumed the possibility is there with marriage & kids - I assumed the opposite.

Whoops!
I've written some questions down & when we head to Fargo today, I'll ask some...

Cheryl:
Yes. And speak up. If you want to be married, say so. You aren't pressuring or forcing him, you are telling him.

Me:
Yes, I've learned that he responds more when I'm sassy & demanding vs. when I'm being pushover-ish.
I've been writing A LOT this morning; it is so therapeutic. Thoughts on paper = uber helpful.

February 18, 2013:

So, he was a major jerky-jerky for the rest of Saturday and most of Sunday. He did put my Savers donations in the pickup without much complaint, and as we headed up to Fargo, he cranked his tunes. I had told him, as he was sort of napping on the couch that afternoon, that I had some questions to ask him. But he didn't seem to care.

Anyhow, fast-forward to us getting off I-29 onto 19th Ave. He says that he'll drop me off. I knew then that he was just being pissy and a dick about it all. I wanted to scream, "Okay, so you wanted there to be a possibility of having a family, but you NEVER SAID anything about that; so, you can be pissed at me for not saying something like that for TEN years?" I feel like that's what it was boiling down to. I wasn't quiet and upset with him for those hours because I didn't want to be a mom = I was torked at his approach, and the fact that HE was mad about something he had never made known. DUH.

ANYHOW (again), we get to BWWs, and he was about to drop me off at the front door. I say, "Please park so I can tell you something." He does, and I say – through effen tears – that after much thought and writing that I am open to the idea of us being parents.

In the back of my mind, though, were still some fears.

Plus, I mean, he called his nephews birth control, and he'd make comments about people's kids. If you say that stuff, the other person is going to ASSUME things. Same goes for marriage which apparently he might be OPEN to as well.

WHAT THE FUCK, DUDE?!?!

I think we ended with me saying how I wouldn't be the typical mom & that after my surgery and after he's been living down here, etc. etc. we should talk about it. I'm open to it; it freaks me out (oh, I talked about feeling unprepared for it, but I've been unprepared for a lot).

So, now we're back on track with feeling okay & normal. He had dinner with us after all, and it was fun. He chatted with my dad about stuff, and I got to chat with my sister-in-law & Alisa, who might have a cancerous cat on her hands.

I can now focus on my TEENY boobies and running more and getting healthy this summer. It'd be nice to lose some weight and then only pack on a small amount if I got pregos. Plus, with the reduction, I'd maybe go from a C/D to a DD during the pregnancy. I think I can say goodbye to F cups and G cups, etc. I really, really hope so!!

We went to the Bison Turf together, too, that night. I hinted at liking to be married before the conception of the child; just because we have family who have conceived out of wedlock, doesn't mean we have to. (We have a choice here.) So, maybe we could elope in the fall and conceive on a teeny honeymoon? Then have a larger reception-y thing over Christmas break? I don't know.

One change, one crazy event, at a time! JEEZUS.

First, a four-day week, then babysitting Audrey, then another 4-day week before surgery and two weeks of healing time.

February 19, 2013:

If I'm really serious about using this surgery as motivation to slim down, then I should start trying to understand why I eat what I eat and why and all that. This morning, I was hungry when I woke up, but that sensation was somewhat gone by the time I showered. I had some water and my multivitamins while doing my hair, and then at about 8:30, I finally had cereal.

I'm not craving coffee right now; I'm sipping on some green tea, actually… 140 calories per bottle. I'm doing lunch with the ASC girls & Anne (I think & hope), so I may try to eat half of the typical lunch servings there OR just get a big salad with chili?

I just have to listen to my stomach & make sure I'm not just eating while bored! And if all else fails, I'll go on Weight Watchers after my surgery and do P90x!

February 25, 2013:

So, it was a crazy weekend with Audrey. Alisa and I did our best to take care of her & have fun with her, etc. I think we did well.

Meanwhile, while she napped, I looked online for blogs by those who had had breast reductions. Some horrible stuff out there, but I suppose I will have bruises and stitches around my nipples. Ew. Ugh. I'll just lube myself up with Aquaphor!

Maybe I should keep a play-by-play, too, of how my process goes. I mean, Shannon said she had her surgery on a Thursday and was back at work Tuesday; that's insane! I'm guessing that my first week will stink, but I'll have to just take my drugs and drink lots of water and rest rest rest.

Yeah. One gal did say that she tried to carry something that was ten pounds too soon, and that that screwed up her one side. So, Jan is a bit right that I should definitely not overdo it.

February 26, 2013:

Nervous.
Excited.
Tired.
Nervous.

They are going to chop my boobs off. Or at least suck fat out of them from the bottom. And then they are going to staple my nipples somewhere decent. And there's gonna be bruising and soreness, and I might barf on my honey-of-a-boyfriend who will be pretty pooped out that day too (last day for him at the bar the night before). And... then there will be these drains that will show my body getting rid of blood and energy and boob juice.

[Note: Never had drains; I failed to ask about that.]

Yeah. Boob juice.

Then they'll have to take the stitches out. [Note: My stitches dissolved or something like that; I failed to ask about that.] And at some point I'll have to look at the itty bitty titties and try not to get upset about them looking like punching bags. Small punching bags, but still. And I'll have to not cry about finally losing a super annoying part of me.

Excited.

I am going to have a smaller chest. Then I'll be able to find fucking bras, and I can wear white button-ups because my back fat won't be as horrible (I'm guessing that with less to lift in the front, the back won't be squeezed to death?) and then I'll be able to throw on random sports bras and do jumping jacks. Good lord, something as simple as jumping jacks. Remember when I took that aerobic class at NDSU, and I was like HOLDING THEM when we did jumping jacks? Jeezus christ.

It may or may not take some getting used to. I don't know. It will feel super strange to lose about three pounds from my front. I wonder if I'll notice when I come out of my haze of anesthesia.

So, if I sometimes feel "tiny" up there in certain clothes now, just WAIT until they are actually chopped down! Holy shit balls.

Tired.

I have been thinking so much about everything. Worrying about really dumb shit – small shit like "Will I be able to put a tampon in because my period comes the week after the fucking surgery?" Yeah. Super dumb crap like that. Or "Will I be able to brush my teeth?" "Can someone come over and put makeup on me?" Yeah. I'm cracked out. And I'm also tired from sleeping fairly well, but then waking up to pee and realizing I can't just sleep on my side come Friday... for probably like a month. That definitely BLOWS.
Yeah... I need to go home and nap. If I get a cold or have a fever on Friday, they won't operate, so I have to take care of me. True story no matter what the time of year, right? RIGHT.

I guess I'm at least glad I am blogging about this. I may or may not publish it on a "live" blog. Yeah.

February 26, 2013 (Part 2):

I have a big nose.
I have big hair.
I have a big chest.

I have no problem being referred to as a bitch. Or the teacher with lots of blonde hair and a big nose. But when it comes to my chest, being the "big-boobed bridesmaid," is no fun. I didn't get to choose them; I do choose my hair shape... and yeah, I didn't choose my nose, but because it's like my dad's, it's easier to be okay with.

My chest does connect me to my mom. That might be an underlying thing that bugs me most about them. Well, actually, the back aches and not finding bras and not being able to run REALLY bug me the most, but she has a large chest; I'm the only girl with a large chest. Even when my sister Robin got preggers, she went up to like a big D, and that's it. Alisa is at a B or C, and has been most of her life.

No wonder I have felt alone in all this. My sisters don't get it, my boyfriend's hands are large (so he liked that mine are more than a handful), and my dad never thought mine were of worry because they are still smaller than my mother's.

And in our society, having big ones is WANTED, like curly hair (from straight-haired girls) and vice versa... then again, that's a common flip-flop; the breast issue isn't... many large girls, from what I've gathered, are okay with them, and small girls want implants. Okay, maybe the large girls want reductions with implants so they are large and perky... but rarely does someone REALLY want Bs or Cs, right? I mean, I can NOT remember the last time a swimsuit top didn't KILL my neck to wear.

I don't know if EVERYTHING I've done has been limited by them. I mean, I did do a Half Marathon with them (and my legs hurt the most from the compression things I wore on my knees), but I was in three sports bras I think. They were suctioned to me by the end. Ick.

And the SMELL. This might be TMI, but when I wear a sports bra for any amount of time, the space between my breasts gets sweaty and stinky – like toe jam kind of stink. Delightful, right? I'm sure that'll continue to some degree with smaller breasts, but I just look at them like these large fatty tissues... that are floppy and weight me down and don't fit into anything.

The 34G bras I bought technically didn't even fit in the cup area. That middle piece was rarely all the way to the skin between my breasts; I'm probably a fucking H right now. Jeezus. And I think I'm more of a 35 around than a 34 or 36, so that complicates things too.

UGH. I recall the last time I was around 200 pounds – at the beginning of Grad School. That weight gain was so different because I was like a 38 around and maybe a D or DD, but when it started to go away, the cups stayed large and I lost fat around my midsection. Strange, eh? Totally. And that was also when I wore size 18 pants... I can't fit into 18s now without them falling off, and I'm back around 200 pounds. So, somehow I gained it all in very strange spots? I mean, my waist is smaller and my legs are too. I guess maybe I was more active for a time there (in between grad school and now), so perhaps I bulked up the muscle underneath the fat now? It weighs more but takes up less space? I don't know.

Stupid body.

Then I went and twisted my left ankle yesterday. It didn't swell, and it felt better after acetaminophen (I can't take ibuprophen this week = totally blows ass) and when I had it elevated...

So, before the boyfriend left today, he equated (in the middle of our conversation about how I'm nervous and don't know what kind of pain to expect Friday) all this to having his appendix out. Okay, sure, that was a major operation, but that's one's stomach and not a woman's BOOBIES with NIPPLES. Yeah! He's a dude.

Whatever.

Okay... I think I'll finish my drink (last one until a week after the surgery I'm guessing) and watch <u>New Girl</u> before reading more of <u>Prairie Silence</u> by Melanie Hoffert.

February 27, 2013

First Dream.

I had my first dream about the surgery last night.

They made them BIGGER. Yeah, in the dream, I come out from "being under" for X amount of hours, and there are massively large boobs hanging from me. And I say, "What the fuck?" And everyone looks at me like I AM the idiot who asked for them. I was super, super pissed off.

And now I'm wondering... where would they get the fat?

February 28, 2013:

So, he was all "I'm gonna quit my job to help you out" for awhile there and just this afternoon on the phone – texted him that I have to be there tomorrow at 5:15am – he switched to "I'll drop you off & come back around noon." I don't want to come "out of it" and not see him soon after. Duh, right? F**king A, man.

And he's not going to come in at the beginning and stay with me until I get settled? I wanted to say "I love you" before I get "wheeled into surgery" for christ's sake. Errrg.

So, now I'm stressed by this whole "what will this surgery & recovery do to 'us'"? And I don't need that added stress. I may just have to tell him what I want; he can't read my melon. And, really, if he disappoints me, then we'll have to chat 'bout that. I'd be by his side for anything like this! It goes back to when I'm sick vs. when he's sick, doesn't it?

There are always too many thoughts in my head. Where's the OFF switch?

Sideboob #2: If I Pass Away...

If I were to pass away during the surgery...

I'd want my life insurance + IRA + 401k + savings + checking to be used:
...first to pay off my debt (student loan through SLND, if necessary) + credit cards (Target) + the house (if it can be paid off with money leftover).
...then give the house to Jan (whether it can be paid off or not); he can sell it to pay off his debt or whatever.
...then use some money for a funeral. I'd want a non-church-based ceremony and a small party after where everyone has to do at least one shot of Grey Goose. Oh, and cremate me, please, and sprinkle me in Sybil Lake in MN.
...then use any leftover money for a trip for my siblings to go to Greenland together. Or Europe.
...if anything is leftover, money-wise, give it to ASAH.
...my sisters (and Hilary) should go through my clothing & books and keep whatever & give whatever away.
...Dad can do what he wants with my bug.

I love you all.
Even if I disliked someone, they still taught me who not to be.
:)

I'll miss my honey. And his kisses & conversation.
I'll miss my Tootie Fruity, bitchy cat.
I'll miss drinking & analyzing life with Alisa, bullshitting with Dad, rolling my eyes at Ma, helping Robin by watching Audrey, telling Jed Apple products are the best, and I'll miss my adopted sisters: Hilary, Fran, Ann, Megan, Cheryl, & KJ who got me through so much.

I'll miss my gay hubbies, too: Mark, Lennie, & Richard.
And I hope Alisa would take custody of Sushi.

Chapter 7: March 2013. (Month One.)

Everything went better than expected w/the surgery & him. I'm swollen, the pain is really just annoying, and I haven't pooped since 5 am yesterday.

I don't recall, at all, going under, but I do know that what lead up to it all was a visit with a pharmacist who told me to stop taking ibuprophen like it was candy (does he have big melons on his chest?), and I took a pee test (my surgeon said that a few of her patients have "discovered" they were pregnant RIGHT before having this surgery – isn't that a waste of time?! And THINK of the shock!) and then they wheeled me into a room with like 5 million lights and 15 people in masks, and right when I wanted to go "balls out" freak out, I was out.

The next thing I knew I was in recovery feeling groggy with blurry vision... an old guy next to me was freaking out, and the sweet nurse was making sure I was hydrated. She eventually had to take my catheter out (weird experience –never had one before), and the oddest thing was that I COULD move my arms. Now I understood the "don't move your arms for weeks after" thing because I legitimately could; I thought they would be sore or something.

We were there at 5:15am & I went into surgery around 8 (under at 7:30?); I was out at 11am & he was waiting for me. My little lady surgeon gave him a pep talk, and he was one big look-of-concern for awhile. But we ordered food together and watched TV in my spectacular room (Sanford had just renovated their "women's wing").

The nerve twinges in my breasts are uncomfortable, and the incisions underneath feel like bra wires rubbing me... ick. I am definitely smaller already even with the swelling; they don't look quite awesome, yet, but I'm already happy that they are a lighter weight. She took a pound from each.

I have to be a T-Rex for a few days and replace the padding in the compression bra everyday; I can take a shower tomorrow if I want, too.

Jan was with me for most of the afternoon, and Alisa came to visit after work. She attempted to put mascara on me, and we laughed at how shaky her hands were. I think we Facetimed with our parents in Arizona, but they were have a cocktail or two and didn't seem as concerned about me in that moment as they had been when they first left for AZ. My dad simply asked what drugs they had me on.

I wanted new, clean undies on. I wanted Malt-o-Meal. I wanted to nap a lot.

Before coming home, we stopped to see (and give keys back) to Robin, Nick, and Audrey. She had just had lunch and told me she had M&Ms. Her little face seemed to be able to tell I was not doing super well.

More later. I just took two pain pills. I weened off the IV yesterday & am taking two hardcore pills every 4 hrs. I had some food yesterday afternoon & a carb-ish breakfast with El Toro soup for lunch at 3pm. I do not have a massive appetite, but that's okay by me. I'm going to be pear shaped, sort of, now.

March 4, 2013:

A Facebook conversation.

Me:
Update: Saw boobies for the first time yesterday in order to change the padding between the compression bra & skin. They are smooshed... looks like they got into a boobie fight with some other boobs and lost. Don't know if I want Jan to see them; they are not pretty, but I know they'll change.

I could've showered yesterday, according to the doc, so I will today. Will attempt to have Jan do my hair or I may go down to the salon in town.

Pain is okay = the nerves cause twinges every so often that really suck, but that means they are trying to get their act together. I'm already down to just one hydrocodone very four hours; using ibuprophen for the headaches BUT NO BACK ACHES! Woot woot.

I've been resting a lot & pretending to "be a T-Rex" as the doc put it. My arms don't hurt, but I can't overextend them until everything is healed up.

I can't wait to sleep on my sides & poop! TMI??

It was awesome to see you last week!

Arielle:
I was just thinking about you when I woke up I swear. I was like-I have to FB Sybil and see how she is doing! Sounds like it's going okay considering!

Good to hear!
When do you have to go back to work?

Me:
March 18: I took sick leave this week & spring break is next week.

Arielle:
Hopefully you'll be all healed and feeling better by then! Speedy recovery. Off to finish getting the Gus man ready for school. It was so good to see you too and thanks again for helping the library out!

March 5, 2013:

Poop. And other things.

Update I sent my gal pals & others via FB yesterday:

Saw boobies for the first time yesterday in order to change the padding between the compression bra & skin. They are smooshed... looks like they got into a boobie fight with some other boobs and lost. Don't know if I want Jan to see them; they are not pretty, but I know they'll change.

I could've showered yesterday, according to the doc, so I will today. Will attempt to have Jan do my hair or I may go down to the salon in town.

Pain is okay = the nerves cause twinges every so often that really suck, but that means they are trying to get their act together. I'm already down to just one hydrocodone very four hours; using ibuprophen for the headaches BUT NO BACK ACHES! Woot woot.

I've been resting a lot & pretending to "be a T-Rex" as the doc put it. My arms don't hurt, but I can't overextend them until everything is healed up.

I told Cheryl via text that I'm already happy about the size, and they will shrink more because they are puffy. When my sis Alisa visited me in the hospital Friday, she said I already looked smaller.

I can't wait to sleep on my sides & poop!

Keep me posted on what's happening with you all; it'll make me feel better to be connected to stuff outside the house!

March 5, 2013 (Part 2):

So, I did officially and FINALLY poop this morning. Twice. Dense lil' turds, but at least I'm getting rid of waste. The body is getting back to normal. Yet, to be honest, this hydrocodone doesn't give me much of an appetite, so that part doesn't have to change. Hee hee!

Just changed the padding an hour ago; took an "after" shot, too, since I took a before one Thursday night. To compare the two is insane right now since bruised smooched boobies are not attractive, but my gigantic G/Hs are not pretty to look at either. I'm probably pushing a D/DD right now (they are sitting very high), but they are very puffy and swollen yet. I probably will end up a C as I requested.

Thus far, I'm needing less and less of the pain meds... my armpits itch, and I still get twinges in each breast, but it's all manageable. I just need the incisions to heal, so I can regain my arm movements... and once they calm down in size, I can purchase underwire bras. I'm already liking the fact that I won't have to worry about bras for the first 3 months; I'm supposed to stick with compression bras or at least ones without underwire. It's nice to wake up and not have to worry about finding a goddamn bra that fits. YAY ME!

I'm looking forward to shrinking down my entire body. This non-appetite thing is a great jump-starter, for sure. And I can't wait to throw on ONE sports bra and go for a run!

*Odd Sidenote: There aren't a lot of stories out there (on like Amazon) about breast reductions... lots about cancer, of course, but I wonder if I wrote up a small electronically-based story on all that I'm going through, if that would be of use to people? I could sell it for cheap, and focus in on my journey = why my large chest didn't seem like an asset to me. Why not every girl wants that kind of attention, etc. ...

I think I need to stop typing for a bit; my right breast feels funky again.

March 5, 2013 (Part 3):

I'm a crackhead. But, like, without the crack.

And I'm an English teacher who doesn't "believe in" Shakespeare. Yeah, he may as well have been Santa. But I had to read everything by him, and all I got was this lousy t-shirt. No, no, no shirt, actually. Just an after effect of freaking out lit majors and starting sentences with conjunctions. Oooh, blasphemy!

Thee above could be chucked into my mini-book about my breast reduction? Or I could use it in my e-textbook? Dunno yet, man.

March 5, 2013 (Part 4):

Today's Ladies:
Very itchy & bruised. Just a few small pin pricks of blood were on the padding from yesterday.

I got uber tired early this afternoon; it could mean the drug sucked me dry or that I overdid it by grading shit this morning. Dunno. But I got teary-eyed before lying down around 5pm... oh, I guess I'm due for my period, too, so there's that as well.

The boyfriend made a late din-din of lasagna tonight; I had two slices & two pieces of French bread, too. He noted that this may be the most I've eaten in one sitting since we got home Saturday. He might be right. "Your body wants to fill up because you pooped." I'm having a Diet Coke which feels strange, too; I've cut way back on this stuff.

This morning: coffee & Lucky Charms (I suddenly crave them!). Lunch: slice of pizza, water, pork chop, beans, and frozen Greek yogurt.

March 6, 2013:

Day 5.

So, I woke up a wee bit light-headed & slightly nauseous at 9am... got downstairs & wiped my face & brushed my hair... the boyfriend woke up and seemed pooped, but worried I'd eaten too much cheese the night before. He gave me a Vitamin Water & lied back down on the couch (he decided to sleep separately from me lazy night so as to not wake me too early like the morning before). I made myself eat cereal, and I headed back up to bed.

I'm watching It's a Brad Brad World on Bravo (my favorite network). I'm realizing that I really miss curling up on my side.

Also realized that I sometime wake up from naps or whatever – I'm like, "Oh, yeah, my boobs got chopped off."

I really want my back scratched today. And a shower because I want to do my hair "the right way" – the little preggers stylist curled some of it towards my face the other day & that's not how I do it. Super shallow, right?

I think I still have to poop more, too. Or I have a gigantic fart in me brewing. Ew, right? Yeppers.

Lessons: I'm not a very patient person. I don't depend on others well...

And, yet, I like that small things make me happy = Say Yes To Blueberries washcloths, pooping, peeing, sleeping on my back that leads to less wrinkles, DQ Blizzards, fish sammies, kissing my honey, how he scolds me about putting my arms down, ...

Tomorrow: I want to wear my awesome sauce sweatshirt, but I need to cut the back open & put ties or buttons on it (easy on off). I need really big men's tees for under my sweatshirts; the zippers will be less annoying I think.

*I wish there was a cute book about someone's journey that I could've read while healing. The basic blog entries are okay, but yeah... I want to record how all this goes = the stories, the reactions of students and family and colleagues.

Yesterday, I missed a text from KJ. She invited me out for a drink. I love her, yet I was kind of upset. I thought, "She knows I can't drink or drive, right?" and maybe she would've picked me up (that's what the boyfriend said, so I think he was semi-okay with it), but it seemed mean to me. Why not come over & see me instead? Dunno. And yet I know that her dept is going through hell, so I feel bad for being even kind of upset. It could be the fucking period I'm about to get, too. Yeah.

Another story: When our mom Facetimed with my sis & I in the hospital, she really didn't seem to care about how I was. I think she said I looked tired and Dad asked about the drugs I was on. They were all drinking in AZ, so yeah. (All this after Mom teared up pre-airplane drop-off a week before.) Thank goodness my sis was there; she understands & made light of it before she tried to put mascara on me (early-onset-Parkinsons hands!).

Only one student blatantly asked what I was having done. I said I didn't want to say. He may have felt guilt & thought my ovaries were taking a hike? I really don't know if students and others will notice? I rarely showed off the massiveness that is WAS my chest... scarves scarves scarves and very lil' cleavage showing ever.

I need to record stories and daily funnies, etc.

—This is the Year of Books and Boobs.
—Last boobie smoosh with Cheryl & KJ.
—The cake Cheryl made me.
—Bill calling my surgery a funeral.

March 6, 2013 (Part 2):

Of course, I can't just heal and rest and read and write at a calm, balanced pace. Oh, no. I have to attempt to write books while I'm in bed. Sheesh. So, I already used my Blogger account to set up two new blogs that will advertise/record the ebook process... Anti-textbook & The Big-Boobed Bridesmaid. Yep.

March 6, 2013 (Part 3):

I'm oddly excited that we are heading up to Fargo tomorrow for my post-op. I'm thinking of what to wear, and I painted my nails a semi-colbalt blue... I think I'm pumped to get out of the house, but also to ask my doctor some questions that I seemed to have forgotten the answers to. Like how long do I have to have padding between my bra and my skin? Or how much should I be pooping now because I've only pooped twice (on Tuesday probably due to the coffee I drank)? Or should I be wearing the bra ALL day? And when exactly could I wear underwire bras? Month 3? I know that she answered some of this, but I DID have a lot of drugs in me the last time I saw her. DUH.

Yeah.
Time to watch the news with my honey in our bed.
Word.

p.s. He just asked me if I ate anything after our subs around 4pm today. I think I ate too much yesterday, so I'm trying to calm it down. It may have caused my nausea this morning, or it may have been my period that did that too, but I don't need to consume a ton of calories. Just good calories and LOTS more water. The Diet Coke I had today didn't make me feel awesome, so... I think I'll return to less of that. It's super cute he's checking up on my diet, however. And wanting me to eat more.

March 8, 2013:

Some of my gal pals from the college (and Megan!) came by today for an hour or two to drink wine (they did; I attempted to have one Stella) and eat popcorn and check up on me. I shared my concerns about people whispering about "why did I have it done" or even "what did I have done" and "gee, she used sick leave for that." Plus, I really don't know if ANYONE will notice. I looked through my Facebook pics, recent ones, and I really DID cover up my chest. In a few pics, I look the same size as my sister & she's a C. I guess I really did disguise them. Scarves and big shirts and minimizers work wonders.

I'm excited that at some point – probably this summer – I will put on a 34/36C bra or swimsuit top. Or just one awesome sports bra and run happily. It will take awhile to get there; I have to worry about padding the lower part of these compression bras for at least a month, so that takes me into April. Hell, I may not even be the size I SHOULD be by the time school starts up in the fall (April 1 = 1 month complete; August 1 = 5 months complete) since she said it can take 3-6 months to completely lose the swelling bits.

Wowzers.

And if we decide to start a family, I'll end up pumping up the boobies soon after. But we'll get to that when we get to that. He needs a back-up plan (job) & I'd like to have the wedding discussion, too, before kiddos even come into our future.

He was a bit distant today, but he can get like that from time to time. He is, AFTERALL, going through a change, too. He's officially moved down here, and he has to adjust to being HERE and being with ME (as non-100% I am right now with healing and such) and not having income, or knowing where to start in order to get more income.

What I tell myself time and time again is that I can not tippy-toe around him. I will not be uncomfortable in my own house. If he's in a bad mood, or just quiet, I don't have to be quiet as well; I can just ignore him and write and read and pin shit on Pinterest. Hells yeah.

My default thought is always that I would be okay without him. It would suck, but if it came down to a massive fight about how we don't have the same future in mind, then I guess we part ways. [...]

Nuff said.

Okay, so the boobies. I showed the girls the bra and padding I'm dealing with. I couldn't hug anyone, and then my parents came by after they were at the bar. He was semi-upset that they gave me drug-taking advice, but overall, it was a good short visit. It sounds like they are heading to Fargo tomorrow, and we have his bro's family coming into town, potentially. I just need a fucking shower in the morning. Oh, and my mom made sure to comment on how small I looked already. Um, I'm wearing a semi-large-ish sweatshirt & it looks like I have a monoboob due to the compression bra. It felt a little pushed or overdone, but whatever. She brought me pretty rings, so I think I can overlook a "fake-ish" compliment.

I tallied up my drug-intake from the week. I was on about 4 a day, of the pain pills, and today I'm attempting to take 3 (with lots of supplemental ibuprophen).

On Monday, I want to start strength training just my lower body. I think by doing a lot of strength training first, my eventual cardio will be easier; I don't know if I've ever "trained" this way. Could be interesting. And I'll keep the workouts to 20min or less; I'm more likely to workout if the time is less than a TV show AND if I vary what I do. If I get bored with what this app called Sworkit gives me, I can use my Sweat It Out board in Pinterest. Duh!

What else do I need to report? Dunno...

I just really, really hope I can keep these boobs at bay from now on. I don't care about my large-ish nose or my butt shaking (in fact, if I could make it less wide but still big-ish & muscular, that'd be great) and Dana today said, "Women are always unhappy with something on them."

As I looked at those pictures of me recently, I did see that I did NOT look like a big boobed giant, but I felt that way. It doesn't matter how I look right now; I'm on the path towards feeling great inside if I'm not there already. It's a relief to have this weight, literally, off my mind now. Daily, I'll just get up now and put on a compression bra and button-down and skinny jeans and cute heels and call it good. No more fighting with bras or tugging at myself all day or having horrible posture or eating ibuprophen for back pain. Ugh.

Fart attack.
My poops are hard, as are my farts. Gotta push & hope they aren't disguised as shits.

Yesterday, I hung out with my family... ended the day with a massive headache after 12 ibuprophen (4 x 3 times) throughout the day. I tried to go all day without pain pill. I took 2 before bed & didn't sleep well at all. Then he started snoring. Ugh.

I guess I am springing forward in a crabby way.

I kept stretching forward in recliner (moved to couch at like 6am); I don't think that that is good for the boobies' incisions! Shoot!

1. I found an amount of blood in my padding this morning that would typically be around the areola part of my new breast... my boyfriend wasn't too concerned – "Let's see how the padding looks tomorrow" – but that was a bit freaky. I bet it was about a teaspoon's worth, but still. I've, up to now, had just little dots of blood around the underside of the breasts (I have upside-down T-shaped incisions).

2. I am in, perhaps, the second stage of how these buggers are going to feel. And that would be sore. Like they already look like they were in battle, and now they feel like they ran half-marathons without me. Or lifted double their weight at the gym one day after a few drinks and woke up like, "Oh my god, why am I sore?" And, yet it could be this bra, they are starting to bounce more. Again, as separated by the commas, it could be this bra; it's the one the hospital sent me home in. The strap was falling apart a bit, so I sewed her up. BUT the other bra from the hospital – beige (ew) – is more sturdy AND the three I found on eBay (different company who makes identical bras with more spandex) are much better quality. Ah, healthcare*. And I bet the ones from the hospital will cost "me" $50 a piece while the ones from eBay were each under $35. Sheesh louise.

*I should clarify that the healthcare I have through the college is amazing; my boyfriend calls it the Cadillac of Healthcare. And it is. This surgery will probably cost $10k+ (overnight stay, etc.), and I'll only end up forking over about $1k. So, I don't know what I'm bitching about... oh wait, I do. The reason healthcare, and this is the most political I'll get I hope, is spendy doesn't really fall on the healthcare insurance side of it; it's crazy what things supposedly cost and that comes from the hospitals and clinics themselves (right?). I mean, I was charged like $90 for a tetanus shot awhile back. This is a required thing every ten years just IN CASE we all fall on top of rusty nails or something; it wasn't covered, so I had to dig deep (okay, not really) for that $90. Half of it was for the "shot" part and the other for the damn nurse to put it in me. My sister-in-law was like, "Um, I could've administered that shot for free." Duh.

3. He seems to be getting more distant with me, yet he does ask if I want help in the kitchen with anything and he asked just now, as I was coming up to bed, if I wanted his help. Like I've mentioned, he's going through his own shit on top of me not being my typical big-boobed independent self.

Normally, we don't see each other on weekends. If I weren't recovering, I'm sure I would've been hanging out with my family more (took a 2+ hour long nap instead yesterday = that's how I know my body is still not back to 100%) and drinking and shopping, etc. Instead, I cut my visit with them short today (they all wanted to get back to Fargo anyhow because the roads suck), so I could rest and shop online.

4. My appetite is barely surviving. I have to force myself to eat, and I'm not saying that like eating doesn't interest me. I really wasn't hungry at breakfast time, so I just nibbled on stuff my parents cooked up. Same with before my 5pm nap; I had lasagna and it was good, but I mostly ate it because I knew my nap would go better if I had food in my stomach with the ibuprophen. I really, really could easily starve myself on this hydrocodone – which I've started taking just at night (started that yesterday) – but the doc was like, "Don't start your diet just yet!"

5. Tried on the ASOS dresses I ordered. Size 14s. All fit (well, I couldn't fully zip up the backs, but they would zip) and all were cute. Yet, I think I could find something under $50 from some place else for Dream$ Auction in April (12th), and... I wasn't completely sold on where the waistlines hit me or the bottom hems (two of them – super cute at the shoulder area – had criss-cross pieces in the front which could lead to unfortunate peeks at my crotch while sitting). HOWEVER, the top parts were a bit big even with my padded chest. It is going to be SO NICE to fit into shit. I lose weight fairly easily in the waist area, and I have no issue with pumping up/toning up my bootie and thighs.

I just have to give all this soreness a few months.

6. I can see how some women get depressed over all this. I don't think, for me, it's sadness over loss. I am glad they are gone. But it's a depression of, "When will I feel 100%?" and "Why did I do this to myself; I don't feel great" and "I hope they look normal at the end of it all" and "What if he doesn't like them?"... Plus, you combine these thoughts with the fact that you can't do what you want when you want (like I want to go to Fergus' Target tomorrow, but I can't really go by myself on this damn drug) and you can't wear what you want yet (reason I just bought way too many shoes on eBay today) and you are so damn tired, TOO.

7. [I like odd numbers, so I'll end with seven.] I had a good conversation with my girls on Friday evening and then with my sister last night while watching TV in our bedroom last night (she curled up on our awesome little sofa chair) about "What if others don't notice?" and "Wow, I really covered them up, didn't I?" and things like that. I normally don't care what others say or think of me – for real, I try to just stick to my own bubble – but I think it's a part of how self-aware I am. I need to prepare myself for what others might say or think. Even if I don't care about what they say or think, it's just good to take in those thoughts and process them. And then shit them out. Hee hee hee.

7.5. Speaking of shit, I really want to poop daily again. It's not happening yet, and so my coffee intake might cause me to massively explode one day. If this happens, someone should fast-forward to this spot and read this part. Then they'll go, "Oh, wow. She died like Elvis." Or something like that. Didn't he die on the toilet? I think my last moments will be that way OR in my bug. And obscenities will be a big part of both.

I'm not sure why I'm so demented, but I did see a piece of Chelsea Handler's interview with Oprah, and O commented on that. That Chelsea was just being her true dirty self, and that's why she was famous and had found an easy gig for herself – she didn't have to act; she is who she is. Amen to women who can be successful and sexy and smart and use the f-bomb and talk about poop.

My List of Things I Need from Target or Walmart:
— Padding (might try panty liners; they'll be thinner and cheaper?)
— Neosporin
— Lucky Charms
— Popcorn (that kettle corn stuff is the bomb)
— Packages of x-large men's tees in grey and black

March 12, 2013:

Mini-Breakdown.

So, this morning, I ended up grading some stuff... via the iPad, which is uber easy & conveeenient (don't care about spelling right now). Then I Facebooked with my gal pals about someone who got let go from campus in a very quiet manner. Creeps me out when they do that.

Anyhow, I went from a relatively chipper attitude, after two ibu for a headache, to lying in our bed trying to nap around noon and crying over every little thing that could pop into my head and turn this whole ordeal into something negative and painful, etc. The boyfriend came up to get the trash from the bathroom, and asked me what was wrong. I just nodded through my tears that it was my tiredness. I'm not sleeping thoroughly enough at night, and getting a heavy two hour nap here & there doesn't cut it.

He left me alone ("Do you want me to leave you alone for a little bit?" I nodded) and then returned awhile later asking if I was hungry. He then fetched us some McDonald's... I have no idea where my need for shakes has come from in all this (as if I was going through a strange pregnancy of giving birth to 2 pounds of fat? Hey, maybe the body wants it back?), but he got me a Shamrock shake and all seemed well with the world.

We went, soon after lunch, to Walmart so I could get more padding (found padding similar to what the hospital sent me home in, or similar to what my doctor gave me = I found 5×9 pads and the hospital gave me 8×10 ones I think). I did get some medium sized panty-liners, too, just in case. They're so cheap anyhow! I grabbed a tube of Neosporin (okay, the generic kind) and XL men's t-shirts and new undies (you can't go wrong with new undies no matter what the occasion) and more Lucky Charms and string cheese and kettle corn popcorn.

The right areola area that leaked blood a bit Sunday night (and then a wee bit yesterday) did leak some more today. The boyfriend claimed I asked him about the leakage last night, but it was Saturday night when I discovered it. I'm fairly positive. But whatever. It's a little blood, and I hope it just stops coming out and instead stays inside and heals all the screwed up parts it needs to. Duh.

That part came up when I chatted with him pre-bedtime just a bit ago. I didn't mean to start crying, but oh well. He says I shouldn't have overdone it this weekend, and even though I really didn't overdo anything, I was more active than I was all last week. He says, "If I had two weeks to do nothing, I would." And here I've been feeling crummy about not being able to do things or to help him, and it had to hit me AGAIN = I just have to take off my independence button and give it all a rest!

Depending on others, ever since college, has been tough for me. I remember Dad giving me gas money or Mom wanting to buy me something for my dorm room, and I just didn't want help. Even when I was a little sick kid, I wanted to hole up in my bedroom and just have people drop off soup every now and then. Oh HELL, I didn't even complain when I had the flu my first week of kindergarten; I just slept all day until the teacher called my mom. Yes, I am a teacher who slept through her first week of kindergarten! Anyhow... there's my update for today.

I had a bit of a mini-breakdown and told him that I did think to myself from time to time, "What have I done to myself?" He said I should ask Shannon – Hil's sis, but she was such a pro about it, "I was in & out on a Thursday and back at work by Tuesday." She's too much of a champ for me. And it's not like I think I'm a big fucking wimp; there's just not a lot out there about what is normal after all this happens. Everyone's procedures are different; doctors are different, etc. And I'm sick of reading blogs (never thought I'd say that) because they are too short ... or there's something else I don't like about them. Too casual, maybe. "Today I did X, Y, Z with my kids and my pain levels are better everyday! Yay!" Ugh. I said to him, tonight, "This is why someone should write a book about this." I shouldn't have to feel alone. Period.

He ended the conversation on a goofy note saying I should just drink in order to sleep (the pain meds – hydrocodone – do not cause me to sleep, but instead give me strange pre-dream daydreams if anything at all), but we don't have "my kind of wine" in the house, I say back.

So, I sucked down the last 4 of my total 12 ibuprophen (my doc said I could take 2400mg? in 24 hours; that's 12 of the basic ibuprophen one can get at good old Target), and now I'm about to read my book and hopefully pass out. I did take a hardcore nap today at 4pm until almost 6pm; KJ had just texted me about having a drink at P's with her and Cheryl. I declined, sadly, and crashed. Probably a good decision for my health, but I don't want to miss out on time with my girlfriends. I want to get back to the activities I once did, and I think I have to be patient for all that = I can start doing that next week perhaps... there will be plenty more "Safety Meetings" around the horseshoe of the bar.

March 12, 2013 (Part 2):

Due to being lazy & also having a crummy day yesterday & because I love odd numbers, I'm going to start some very simple & easy & fast strength training tomorrow (3.13.13 – surgery was on 3.1.13). I think three exercises at about 20 reps should do it. All leg/ass moves tomorrow with ab shit Thurs. Tomorrow: glute bridges (two kinds) with squats. Thurs: bike crunches, push up crunches, & ? Almost all exercises can be done on my back = better for the boobies.

So, every other day, some very simple/easy/quick stuff to get my body somewhat ready for running in a month...

Haven't taken any ibuprophen or pain pills yet today... and I slept a wee bit better. And I showered today. Sleep and shitting and showering. Yay!

March 13, 2013:

Nip Nip.

Attempting to "nip out" as my body did last night – wine run with the boyfriend – really is a new painful situation for a chest that doesn't have secured nipples. Yeah. Then it got chilly in bed last night, and once again, I flinched. Strangely, about 10% of the pain is pleasurable because it's dealing with a typically pleasure-filled area. Yeah. Yet, I was happy when the "nipping out" attempt would subside. Eeeek.

Just did my tiny workout. Felt "the burn" on that small amount of reps. Yikes.

The spotting in the right areola area is diminishing; the doc mentioned some glue that would start to come off & that that was normal and to use Neosporin on those spots. I've been, since getting the Neosporin, lubing up the areolas before putting padding on. I'm intrigued to try this Bio Oil on the scars once they are healed completely.

I had a semi-daydream last night about wearing a cute pink bra (the one I'm "watching" on ebay that has no underwire) & the boyfriend is like, "Yay, you're showing them off!"

March 13, 2013 (Part 2):

Alone.

So, he went to Fargo to fetch the last of his stuff around 6pm (will return Fri morning, or, I'm guessing afternoon). I went to Walmart after he left... alone & it felt great to drive my lil' bug again; plus, the seatbelt didn't bother my chest (many bloggers mentioned that it would; German cars are just made better?).

I get to Walmart & immediately get a headache. I hate that place, but at least I got out & about!

I graded a wee bit more today, too, and did some laundry.

I can tell he really wants to have a more organized home, so as I feel better, we'll have to get on that. I'd love to chuck a lot of stuff... coats downstairs, purses in storage, scarves, etc.

Earlier in the day:

"So, T wants to meet up with me Friday; I think she just wants to talk about breaking up with the doc."

"Okay. Why are you telling me this?"

"So you know what I might be up to Friday."

"Do you want me to tell you to not go or should I say, 'That sounds good'?"

"Yeah, just say that." I can feel tears forming; why does he have to act like a jerk one minute & then the next minute he's making me dinner and worrying about my pain level.

"I suppose you should get out more," he turns from inconsiderate boyfriend to concerned, "Are you going to be ready for school on Monday?"

Tears well up. I'm too emotional, perhaps, but I've taken two birth control pills in the last two days in order to catch up (my insurance letter expired/my doc in Wahpeton had to resend saying my pill should covered) and ALL of this is new. Plus, when he says that, I think: "Well, if I'm not ready, then I'll look like a wimp."

I tell him that later in the afternoon. I also say that Monday is my longest day; the rest of the week is quiet. He takes me through it, "What can't you do on your own yet?" I mention putting on my coats (my officemate will offer help, I'm sure) and carrying ten pounds and reaching up for things. He role-plays a student asking me why I need help pulling a projector screen down. I didn't have an answer; I don't know if I want them to know?

The "surgical" glue on the right breast – at the cross of the upside-down T – is coming off, so I lubed it up (and the areola) with Neosporin today. And I don't know if the house is colder, but my chest keeps attempting to nip out. Painful & strange feeling!

March 13, 2013 (Part 3):

Boob Book Stuff.
—My other appointments: being told my hemoglobin was 13.1 which is perfect. "Can I have t-shirt that says that?"
—Buying many shoes on ebay because they'll fit no matter if I'm swollen or not. God bless shoes; they make all situations better.

March 13, 2013 (Part 4):

Glue.

Just had to rearrange the padding before bedtime; the glue is definitely coming off the underside of the right areola and at the cross of the upside-down T under the breast (which is a little hard for me to see, but yet I could never see the underside of my Gs!). So, I disinfected a tweezer and pulled some of the excess off before applying tons of Neosporin again. I should've purchased another tube of that stuff, but oh well. I can always get more!

Decided to double-up on the padding (5×7) using tape; it's more comfortable to put excess under the bra band & yet still cover up the areola/nipple. I don't really care, and my shopping spree on ebay lately has proven this too, how much I spend on feeling normal/okay. If I have to use two pads on each breast everyday, oh well! I'm going to be comfortable through all this, damn it. Besides, the padding the doc gave me was supposedly $1.50 a pad & these are 12 for $5 at Wallyworld. I did buy another box today, just because.

I just realized I left clothes in the dryer. I have no ambition to go and fold them up. I want to get into my bed since the boyfriend won't be hogging it tonight and just relax and read that crazy memoir about the drag queen with the boob globes full of goldfish. Yes, he existed.

Oh, p.s., remember how I said there aren't a lot of stories out there about women who aren't uber happy with their large boobs (and how they have reductions without signs of cancer); well, I finally read the rest of this magazine I got at Stop-N-Go awhile back – it's from the UK (yeah, our little ND town had a magazine from the UK... called Easy Living I think?) – and a story in the back is about a women who was small and prayed for boobs when she was little and then was like CRAP, take them back, etc. She turned out to be a 34D (and was okay with it because when she got pregos, they exploded) for most of her life... but she brought up great points: that dudes stare at them and comment on them and that clothes don't fit and that they make you look large if you don't dress them right and... anyhow, it was comforting. I read it thinking, HELLS YES!

Okay. Bedtime!

March 14, 2013:

Sore.

Woke up sore & stiff again. The left breast now has a stinging sensation to it; the right breast looks like it "took" most of the Neosporin "in" last night, and so when I changed padding just a few minutes ago, I lathered them both up with the Neosporin and, since I'm by myself in the house today, I tried out using panty liners for under the breasts along the big incisions... um, I totally could've gotten SKINNIER & SHORTER ones, but oh well. They definitely are comfortable, and the sticky part helped me when I had to clasp everything together.

I really want to sleep on my side; it's almost defeating to get ready for bed, and read, and then try to find a cozy spot for my head because I like to turn my face (to give the feeling of sleeping on my side?).

Anyhow, I haven't done my little workout yet today, but I think with the boyfriend gone, I won't be "forced" to eat a massive lunch and dinner, so if I skip it and end up doing some grading and crafting, that might be enough "exercise." At least it's not just sitting on my butt... wait, I could do quad exercises on the couch using the recliner part! And I just remembered that it's my ABs day anyhow; I can do those this afternoon before a nap or something.

Okay... so I think I'll attempt to grade the small things in my other two f2f classes (kind of glad I assessed the 10am Ag class already because they had the most little assignments due to me seeing them 4 times a week rather than 3) before I try to make Amy's baby shower gift. I plan to create unique onesies for her (and Hil) using iron-on sheets and iron-on letters.

After all this stuff, I think I'll continue to watch the Housewives of OC marathon. Why not?

March 14, 2013 (Part 2):

Pus.

I just remembered one blogger's post I read awhile back about how she bought an ice-pack-bra or something for the swelling, but she didn't need it because she didn't swell up at all. She mentioned that a few times, and I thought, "Gee, way to rub it into those who do, dumbass."

Anyhow, I checked my padding tonight – it's strange to me that I've looked at my chest WAY more than I ever did, like it was that annoying that I tried to ignore the largeness of it – and I had a little chunk waiting for me in the padding near the right breast's areola. Yep, that damn right boob strikes again. This time, it wasn't drips of blood, but pus.

So, tomorrow morning, I'll call Erica (the nurse, since I'm thinking the surgeon will be in surgery?) and make sure this is normal. The areola looks like it did yesterday; I think that Neosporin crap is getting in there and causing things to attempt to heal. Pus ain't all bad, is it? Some other blogger said she ended up with a lump of pus after her surgery, so this stuff can build up... yay?! But at least my boob's getting rid of the pus. Go Boobie?!

I did a lot more today, which could be a good thing and bad thing... and could've caused the pus to get pushed out? Laundry, made onesies for Amy's baby shower, graded some stuff, etc. I took some ibuprophen this morning, and then just about a half hour ago. They are still achey and sore and jiggle just a wee bit (enough for me to notice); all these things cause discomfort. But I'm assuming that discomfort will slowly disappear... I'm hoping that by week 6, I can sleep on my side and just wear padding underneath them?

Yesterday, I think I complained about the leftie starting to ache, and I did notice that this morning, but it went away. I'd love to wake up and not go, "Oh, yeah, I had my boobs chopped off." How do I forget this stuff?

p.s. I was thinking today about wearing bras with smaller shoulder straps. It made me happy to think I might be "one of those girls" who could wear tank tops with little straps that peek out. It IS amazing how many little things I'm looking forward to.

March 17, 2013:

Yesterday in stream-of-consciousness-style = I biffed it going to FedEx. Not cool. I had lunch with Megan, hit Family Dollar, had drinks with Taya (3 of those bad boys!), listened to the boyfriend saying he'd wipe some job with his degree (well, you didn't with the bar job?)...

Today (in more stream-of-consciousness style because I can't type well on the iPad): Attended baby shower, told Hil about how Jan said I should call Shannon (Hil's oldest sister), but I didn't want to seem wimpy; Shannon was shocked my twinges started earlier than hers. Huh.

I asked my cousin Devin if I looked smaller & everyone chewed me out – maybe it was inappropriate, but I am, and I wanted validation since no one cares to give it to me, and it's not like guys don't notice that stuff; and he's practically our brother! Hell, I noticed his strange hair style & told him to buzz it – guys get weird about balding, so I was probably inappropriate in asking him about that too! Whatevs.

I zonked out on drive home with parents; like, the car ride seemed seven minutes long... that's how "out cold" I was, but I was up too early again.

Leakage is way down from previous days: I thanked the boyfriend for letting me freak out about that. Then I asked aloud why the hospital bras they gave me were less cozy than the ones I found on ebay. I went and ordered two more before hand-washing the other two. I like clean stuff!

Before coming up to read, he said he might not cash my check (gave him $550 for X-mas and B-day – long story) & then said something about spending it on me? Weirdo. Change of attitude from night before, I'd say. Right as I got settled up here, he brought up my ibuprophen & fresh ice water. So nice...!

I think I have more to say about both days, but I am beat... need sleepy!

Growing Lumps. Or lumps of growth?

Sitting at the Fryn' Pan today – about to order pancakes! – I feel this phantom lump in leftie. I had already gone to pee, but I headed back to the bathroom anyhow. Nothing suspicious. Huh. I have phantom lumps once in awhile; they are a crazy counterpart to the non-nipping-out sessions.

Both still feel like they could have pieces of fake boob in them; when poked, they barely bounce or move. I'm starting Week 3 here, so I hope all bruising goes down & this damn glue takes a hike.

Just a few min ago, in my nightly prep of lube, I saw that the glue on the underside of leftie's areola wants to come off. This time around, it leaves a crevice though & I try to smooch the boob together as if it's going to split down the center before my eyes... a brownish, syrupy liquid comes up with the glue & I don't pry too hard. OCD-ers might insist on getting all the glue up at once. Not me. It keeps the titties together! Or so I tell myself. I wipe the tiny tidbits of liquid & practically pour Neosporin into the teeny crevice. Heal up, bitch! This is my prayer. I can see that once this glue & the stitches dissolve (or get removed? I should've asked more questions! didn't know about her not using drains, etc.) – because rightie has a few spots that are not glued now – the scars/incisions look less intimidating. Thinner in size, except for crevice man, and much lighter in color. The glue peels up blood, etc. too & that shit is dark when dry!

And we are under a blizzard warning for tonight through tomorrow night; I kind of hope we get another storm day, but I doubt it. I could use one more rest day & even with campus open as normal, my students will skip anyhow.

They closed campus minutes after I zonked out; the boyfriend came up to tell me & I confirmed it on my phone (noti-find system). I woke up at 3am thinking I had dreamt it all; I haven't been able to sleep since. I talked to the boyfriend a bit (he barely kissed me goodnight twice – wth?) & had cereal. When I lied back down, he came to bed, and I couldn't zonk back out. So I came downstairs to watch Housewives of Atlanta & listen to sushi hack/cough.

So, even though I can't sleep, it's all good because I can nap later... this storm day is going to screw up my schedule with f2f classes, but oh well. I'll smoosh stuff into other days.

I almost wanna leave grading for tomorrow (Tues), too, so my arms do less & heal more. I think I'm still hungry!? WTF.

I zonked out around 6:30am or so, woke briefly at 8:30am to see that Sanford (Erica – had called her Fri about the spots I was finding in my padding) was calling. I ignored it & slept until almost 10:30. I feel pretty well-rested, and a bit hungry.

I just changed padding, added lube, & took an updated photo = bruising is less than last shot (taken? first full week home?) and the swelling has maybe gone down a tish...

Today, I'll try to do very little. I can't pass up one more lazy day of healing, can I? Thanks, Ma Nature!

Channel 118.

It doesn't come in on our two smaller TVs (kitchen & master bedroom), so when the boyfriend woke up and took over the remote (as usual), I gave up watching The Rachel Zoe Project (reruns). Granted, I was grading on my iPad, but still.

I am super annoyed with him today. I almost wish we would've had school; I might have reached my "me+him only" time limit which is two weeks. That's a fairly long time.

I wonder... will he sit around all March & not look for a job? And how do I bring that up?

When will we have the chat about babies? In 6 months when I'm healed? Will I get to enjoy the small boobies just a little bit before they get a bit larger due to pregnancy? Huh.

If I had one at 37 (keep thinking I'm older than 36 right now & I don't know why)... I could do one more before 40, right? I wish we could just have twins (or maybe I shouldn't wish that?) or maybe we'll have one of our own & adopt another? I don't know if I'd want only one... I like having siblings A LOT. If we had one when I was 40, I'd be 58 when they graduated; that's not too old really... he'd be 60 (learned recently he's lost two uncles now; they were in their 60s when they passed = Yikes!).

This is too much thinking for one day. TOO TOO much.

Back to watching <u>Sex & The City</u> when Carrie doesn't know if she wants babies with the Russian.

March 19, 2013:

Me:
Hey VB crazies: I just wanted to tell ya'll, privately, that I had breast reduction surgery two weeks ago... SO I may not be totally ready to sub this summer. I'll see what my surgeon says... I hope I get the okay, but I just wanted to give ya a heads-up.

M:
Hopefully you can still be our favorite fan, if you can't play right away.

Me:
Totally!! I love coming to watch & cheer & drink!

S:
And enjoy no snow.

M:
Don't forget the seeds! Oh how I'm missing summer. Hope it's not much longer for the snow to start going away.

Sideboob #3: Follow-Up Questions...

Questions for Follow-Up Appointment:

---How to help swelling go away faster?
Answer from surgeon: Drinking all the water in the world won't help. It goes down on its own time.

---Sleep on side?
Answer from surgeon: If you are wearing a compression bra to bed, yes, you can sleep on your side.

---Three month mark = might be able to wear underwire without padding?
Answer: Wait until 6 months to wear underwire bras (I was given the okay at Month 5).

---Warning signs I should watch for?
Answer: You're doing well. Try not to worry.

---Nipping out = will that ever be normal?
Answer: No. Your nerves are goofy now.

Chapter 8: Mid-March 2013, Back to School.

So, yesterday was my official first day back to work/campus after the surgery... and it went well. My Mondays are typically crazier, but with a snow day deleting all that, my first day was Tuesday, and I only taught one class and had two meetings. I didn't realize how perfectly I had planned my whole surgery; everyone was coming back to the same chaos I was since we just had Spring Break last week.

I got to campus around 9am; it was also awesome to drive my bug to campus since before my surgery, I had my parents' dumb car. Everything feels more normal when I'm in my bug. Wearing a seatbelt is a challenge, so I have illegally not worn it (just plugged it into its latch & that's it)...

First person to see me = my department chair, Wade. He welcomed me back, we vented about students and talked about mythology – I had found this image on Pinterest that I thought would be of interest to him for his class – and it was a good start. I was waiting to hear from my surgeon's office about my appointment on Thursday; I had asked them to move it to the afternoon so I could have my 10am class (missing Monday screwed up a lot of teachers' schedules!).

My class went well; many students showed up and were ready to present (I had to introduce a project online before break, and some had finished them up already!), so that was cool. No one asked how I was, and no one commented on my absence. We talked about the next few weeks, and they went on their merry ways.

After that class, I returned to my office to see that my officemate had brought me flowers. So pretty & so sweet of her. She had, while I was "out," emailed me to check on me and had said before I left that if I needed anything to email her & Wade. I have a great little bunch of colleagues & department members!

I think I did take four ibuprophen that morning and four in the evening; I figured that would be expected. More moving around = more aches... more phantom tumor pains, too. I had one this morning driving to work. It really feels like a little lump of something has formed in the breast and is causing a very specific area of pain. They are fewer and farther between, but still. Damn healing nerves! Get your acts together!

I think I munched on lunch in my office (leftover pizza = the best), graded some things (I made a list of things I have yet to catch up on; I figured I would try to check off something each day, and that seems to be just the right amount of stress to put upon myself right now), talked to Cheryl (she checked up on me, too), and then walked to my 1pm and 3pm meetings... We had a quick pow-wow at 5pm for Math Olympics, and I had two drinks while we discussed that stuff. When I got home, the boyfriend was in full cleaning mode upstairs, so I hung out up there while he was doing things. I think I had a strange dinner of ice cream (lactose free), Muscle Milk, and peanuts. I like to have protein and carbs at every meal – always have.

Today is going well. I have afternoon classes on Wednesday, so I came in at 9am to start grading things and to catch up on a variety of other things... Bill brewed some coffee, so I just put that in my system along with four ibuprophen.

Other thoughts:

-It's strange how much our arms are connected to our chests. I mean, I know they ARE, but the muscles all work together, and when you are large-chested, I don't think you notice it as much. My arms have been about as sore, at times, as when I was in tennis in high school.

-I had to adjust my damn bra/padding yesterday about three times in the bathroom. I did worry that someone would pop in and wonder why I had padding & a strange bra on...

-When I was in bed last night, I adjusted my bra while lying down, and it seemed to make it feel more comfortable. I have been putting the padding in the bra while standing up, and it's probably not allowing me to get them comfortable positioned in there. Huh.

-Last night, at the Math Olympics pow-wow, KJ said us three should go have a nice dinner once I'm really healed up, and I could wear something cute. I have great, great friends.

-I asked the boyfriend last night, "So, you haven't really said much about looking at them?" He said, "I figured it wasn't really up to me." Well-played. It is kind of up to me, and they are looking less war-like everyday. I'll be so happy when they "fall/droop" a bit into the ski-slope shape the surgeon mentioned. Right now, their shape reminds me of a strange-shaped implant. As if the implant is deflated, fat-tire-like, but still hard-ish.

-I also showed the boyfriend a catalog of pretty bras I could buy... he said, "You can't quite wear those yet, can you?" He's very in-tune with how long this will take, and did ask me how my first day went, too... in fact, when I got tuckered out around 9:30pm, instead of later, I said that my first day must've tired me out. He agreed.

-I am still not sleeping uber well in the mornings. I like zonk out on my back well, but once he comes to bed, in the early-early morning hours, suddenly, my body isn't cozy anymore and it wants to be on its side. Ugh. I'll have to ask her how long I have to do that. I'm sure Week 6 is the magic time for that too, just like the running?

-The sand VB team I sub for some summers chatted on Facebook yesterday about being excited for that to start (in like 2-3 months yet! Crazies!), so I did message them my "condition" and said that I thought I could sub this summer, but that I would have to check. And I think it's good they know that I had that done, so they understand why I won't chest bump people or something. Sand VB can get rough.

March 20, 2013 (Part 2):

Just upgraded with $25 for a year's worth of premium on my private blog so when a year has passed, I can take the archives (free download with premium) & make 'em into the book.

So... here's a comical aspect to all this for ya: I saw my breasts via my Photostream today, & I almost accidentally posted one of the pictures to Facebook! I had clicked to add a photo on Facebook using the iPad & when I saw it, I clicked on it because I wanted to delete it... But then I was like, "No, no, NO!" Unclick. What a close call, ya'll! Shit shit shit!

Anyhow, I've noticed that some people don't know what to say when they find out about the surgery. My boyfriend's mom said via email: "I'm glad to hear things went well for you. Now just take it easy and enjoy being waited on and not having to do anything." And my Gma today said: "Hope you are feeling better after the surgery." I mean, I know my non-friends are probably not going to say, "How are your titties?" But it's very long-distance-y if that makes sense. If I had something more serious, would people ask more questions? Then again, when my brother & sis-in-law were having "getting pregos" issues, we tippy-toed around them a lot.

I don't know what I expect. At lunch the other day, before Amy's baby shower, I didn't talk a lot. I actually noticed that I had things to say, but never got the opportunity to speak them. I did tell Hil about my mini-breakdown, and I recall Jed asking about my boyfriend or something, but I was relatively quiet. It wasn't as bad as after my mammogram when no one asked about it (well, Hil might have?), but this non-inquiry really upset my boyfriend. Everyone chatted about their upcoming trips that night, and I was about to get chopped up.

Maybe people think I'll come to them for advice? Maybe they are uncomfortable? Maybe it's a combo?

The strangest reaction might be when our mom got teary-eyed before they left for Arizona, and I recall her being semi-upset that I scheduled it for when they'd be gone. What the hell?

March 22, 2013:

FB Msg to my gal pals:

My follow-up appt when well yesterday; she gave me the okay to sleep on my side. WOOT WOOT. So I did last night, and I feel more rested... even though the sides of my chest are sore. She says I'm healing very well, and I don't go back to see her now for a month. By then I might be able to think about wearing real bras... maybe.

—

Yesterday, before my 2pm appointment, I dropped off a bag at Savers & shopped. I may have overdone it because my arms and chest were sore after, but I tried to take things off & on very carefully. Anyhow, I walked out of there with a few cute things. Right before registering for my appointment, my sister calls me for the second time – means something is up – and she had just gotten fired that morning. Jeezus christ. She wanted to know if I was heading home after my appointment because she was heading there to tell ma&pa.

So, I get in for my appt. The surgeon says everything's healing well, etc. I can sleep on my sides – yay! – and I asked about any warning signs I should watch for from here on out. "No," which makes me think I'm three weeks in, and IF things were going to go to shit by now, they would have. I also ask if there is anything I can do – drink more water? – to get the swelling to go the fuck down. "No," she says. Before her & the little nurse head out, I ask about her conference, and they both apologize for someone not returning my call last Friday – a receptionist had her last day, and messages got lost. It was nice of them to apologize so much; they really didn't want me to freak out. But I said that the boyfriend was like, "If you were infected, you'd have a fever. Calm down."

The doc said, "Sometimes, you just need someone will common sense around you to keep things less emotional." She's a smart one. If anyone I know ever wants to have this surgery done, I will totally recommend her*. I like her a lot. And Erica, her sidekick nurse, too.

*Pamela Antoniuk out of Fargo, ND.

I don't know if I mentioned this on here yet, but I got my bill from Sanford, and it was like $25k for all this shit. What do I owe? Nothing it seems. In fact, the billing said $-200... weird, right? The boyfriend said, "I would just wait to see what happens with that." My deductible wasn't fully used, nor was some other weird insurance thing (left on deductible = less than $400 + other thing, $700 = $1k)... I'd love to get PAID for my boobies, that's for sure, but I think something hasn't been calculated or whatever. Like our dad says, "We'll see."

The boyfriend headed up to Fargo last night for the F/M Walleye Club. He said, "I always wanted to go, but I had to work," so now he's got a new thing. I'm happy for him. Oddly, when we almost bought this other house a few years back (long story on what happened with that one), he said, when I wanted to go to my sister's birthday party after we would've moved in, "You know, we won't be going to Fargo as much after this," and yet we are now. And I'm fine with it, but it's funny how he went from wanting to cut ties with anything up there years back to now... people DO change!

March 22, 2013:

A Facebook conversation...

Me:
Hey R = I thought I should clarify the body issues a wee bit: I just had breast reduction surgery three weeks ago... so once the girls heal and I can start running and biking again, I will feel pretty awesome. Just have to be patient with this thing called healing.

RD:
Ouch...been there done that!! Sorry if I got crazy...I'm just all bout nurturing, girl power, hail to the V kinda thing...lol

Me:
No, no problem at all. I'm usually so much more positive about my body, but right now, I can't even sleep the way I want to,... I'll get back to "me" though. Have a great weekend!!!

RD:
I was holding my boobs down when I drove...good luck, and wowza, we got 30k boobs.

Me:
I almost walked to class holding them today. The doc gave me the okay to sleep on my sides last night (thank god), and so now I'm better rested yet my sides are so sore. Oh well.

RD:
Wait till the nerves start doing their thing...oh & u swear I have "ghost" nipples! Hahaha where they used to be!

Me:
Oh, the nerves have been having parties in certain spots for all three weeks now. I call the parties phantom balls ... and I wish my body would stop trying to "nip out" = uber painful.

When did you have the surgery completed? Did they have to take off a lot?

RD:
I had it about 8 years ago...3lbs each...or close to it...best thing I ever did

Me:
Wow. I "only" had a pound taken out of each... already, my back is so happy. I should've done this sooner, but my family was like, "You're not that big." Um, okay, weirdos.

Have you seen much change in size since?

RD:
Haha how would they know? Not really other than w/ age...little saggier?

Me:
Gotcha. I'm still swollen, but the doc says I'll be a C/D. I hope I never see double letters ever again.

RD:
He told me there was no size for me! But was also heavier then...best part was buying a cute/sexy bra!

Who was your doc!

Me:

Pamela Antoniuk. She's the bomb. Just saw her for my follow-up yesterday. I can't wait to buy a PINK bra.

RD:
Ah...I had [Dr. X]...good guy but an odd ball...look out Victoria's Secret!

Me:

I don't think I've ever bought a bra there. Not even in high school. Thanks for the chat, R. It's so nice to run into women who have experienced this & hear their stories.

RD:
No prob! When I see ya next I'll tell ya the "rest" of the story...pretty funny! Have a fabulous weekend!

Me:
Ditto!!

March 23, 2013:

I'm itchy; they're itchy.

But I didn't wake up sore or stiff (or as sore or stiff as the past three weeks), so we're on our way, kids! Plus, it's 2pm, and I just took my first two ibuprophen of the day. They might be the only ones I need, so that would be a major improvement; each day I've needed at least 6-8.

"They" got us out of an event tonight. There's a "Throw Back Prom" event at Legends tonight. I'd normally be up for that, yet I know my boyfriend would not... so when I ran into SR at the thrift store today, I could honestly say I just wasn't up for being that active quite yet. He had hernia surgery around the same time I had my surgery, and he also showed off his latest tat.

Speaking of the boyfriend, for a minute there yesterday, when the kitchen saw dishes sit there for 1/2 day (big whoop right?), I thought he had had enough of "taking care of me." He had hit his limit of being the caretaker for three weeks. BUT he thought he was coming down with a cold, etc., but today he says he's feeling better. He made me an awesome lunch (pork chops & baked taters), so perhaps I was just thinking negatively about him.

[Oddly enough, he claims the Walleye meeting he went up for moved elsewhere. I see that the web site does say Doublewood, but the Facebook page says Kelly Inn. Huh. Either way, he said it was depressing to go back up there and go to the bar & not see many people, etc. Maybe this will encourage him to move onto something that he really enjoys with a social group he can be a part of!]

Today, after hitting two thrift stores and eating, I'm digging into making garland/bunting for Hilary's baby shower. I found uber cheap streamers, too, as back up (or in addition to my garland). I think if I get tired of all this, I'll just narrow down my efforts to a big banner that says "Boy Oh Boy" or something like that.

I tried on, and purchased, two sweaters and a top today that I don't think I would've fit into before the surgery. It's strange but cool to fit into things differently; as spring hits, I think I'll see how my dresses from last spring/summer fit and donate as necessary... plus, now that I know how to use this damn sewing machine, I could take in some stuff.

This week: ND Women's Rally (the legislature is trying to pass some extreme abortion bans) in Fargo with Taya Monday night; Melissa's Lia Sophia party Wednesday; Karaoke with that crazy Wateland crew on Good Friday.

March 24, 2013:

A Facebook conversation with Fran:

When is your surgery???? I miss you too!!!!!!!!! Hope you are staying warm over there!

Love you lady!!
-Fran

My Response:

Surgery was three weeks ago, and in my drugged up state two weeks ago, I thought I had emailed you about it all! Silly me!

The surgery went well, & now I'm trying to patiently heal. Jan has been by my side ever since; he won't let me do much & I'm not supposed to lift 10+ pounds or be too active for one more week.

At first, I was in bearable pain & only had one mini-breakdown (they just looked so horrible – like they'd been in a boobie war & lost); now, I'm just uncomfortable & looking forward to the swelling going down & wearing normal bras.

The doc says I'm healing well & it sounds like after three months, I might be able to resume most activities (running/swimming) & wear things with underwire?

Daily, I lube them up with Neosporin & have to remind myself not to hug people like I usually do. They still look like weird implants to me (due to the swelling), but the incisions/scars are fading! She says I'll be a C cup, and I was about a 34G/H before. Even with pregnancy or major weight gain, my chest might only go up one cup sze because those fat cells are all screwed now.

The pain is mostly the nerves trying to get their act together. I call them phantom balls of pain... and I can't "nip out," but my body tried to! Ugh!

So yeah... I'm back to school & I hid my chest so well beforehand that no one has noticed! I hope you & Josh are doing well! Miss you both & thanks for checking in on me.

Love,
-S

March 24, 2013 (Part 2):

Picking at Scabs.

Okay, so I didn't tell the boyfriend, but before I went out last night (for about 3.5 drinks – home around midnight), I picked at the criss-cross T spot under my right breast. I was using a small mirror to see what was going on there, and there was this little something that I thought was glue. Pulled on it... and then decided it was attached and thought I'd just use a clipper to clip off the dangling piece. It started to bleed just a tish, so I wiped it down (with soap) and dried it before chucking Neosporin on it. When I returned from being out, I checked it all out and it had stopped bleeding, leaving a tiny bit of blood (mixed with Neosporin) on the padding.

So, no more picking scabs. I don't need to fuck up anything with these incisions or cause the scars to be larger than normal.

Before zonking out last night, I used my phone to go online and look up breast reduction swelling because they just felt larger yesterday even though I know they haven't gotten larger... there was a long list of people who had posted to this one person's freak out over the swelling she was going through (she wanted to go from a DD to a C & only a few days after the surgery, she was a D = yes, key phrase is "a few days after the surgery"), and the comments were very helpful. One person said they had personally been a nurse, like my Erica, at a plastic surgery place, and they had seen swelling for weeks after for almost everyone! So reassuring. So I bookmarked that site. Maybe that's a piece of advice I could give those who read this book (if it gets made) before their surgery; ask yourself what you feel you might freak out about and look up comments... I wouldn't look at pictures or any horror stories, but find places where people have left COMFORTING messages. I know reading those before bed was so helpful.

Yesterday, I did need 5-6 total ibuprophen. After our mom's singing event today at 2pm, I did take four ibuprophen, but that's it so far for the day.

I slept well, and did curl up on my sides a few times. I'm hoping that the side sleeping doesn't encourage the swelling. At this point, I have to remind myself that if the doc says it's okay, it's okay. She'd tell me if she thought me sleeping on my side would bring on more swelling. I get these thoughts in my head, and I need to calm them down.

Taya did say last night that I looked smaller & when my sis stayed over last Thursday, she said that in my compression bra, I looked smaller than even when I wore two sports bras before. I know it's silly, but hearing others' perspectives does help. It's like during weight loss; when I notice someone's pants getting baggier, I feel that telling them that might help them a wee bit. It's reassurance, and that's what a lot of us want on a daily basis.

March 24, 2013 (PART 3):

CF:
Sybil: what did you have surgery on?

Me:
I had my boobs chopped off.

CF:
Seriously????

Me:
Yeppers. Haven't announced it on FB... and no one has noticed cuz I hid them so well (I guess).

C:
What???

Me:
No one on campus noticed, I should clarify; my friends & fam know.

CF:
So was it a reduction or some kind of preventative surgery because of cancer genes?

C:
Did you get a cancer diagnosis?

Me:
Goodbye Gs... hello to Cs in a few months, after swelling. Oh, yeah, no cancer = should've said that. Sorry.

C:
You scared me!!!!!!!!!!!!

CF:
Me too!!!!!

Me:
Did have mammogram to check, though. Sorry!

CF:
Wow, I had no idea you had Gs! You must have hidden them well.

C:
In this case you should have sent the extra tissue my way.

CF:
Ha!

Me:
Not the first person to ask, C!

C:
But I'll bet I'm the flabbiest!

Me:
Yes, back issues were pissing me off

CF:
You'll have to buy lots of new clothes!

Me:
Maybe; or use sewing machine to take 'em in.

C:
I seriously pictured you with absolutely no boobs. Like just the scars and stitches. I freaked out.

Me:
They look like hell right now. Like they got into a fight with other boobs & lost.

CF:
Has Jan been taking good care of you since the surgery?
BOOB FIGHT!!!!!!

C:

LOL!!!!!!!!

Me:
Sorry I didn't clarify the cancer thing... Yes, he's been a great nurse.

CF:
Jan the murse.

Me:
Why is it that I know only one person who had breast cancer & 17 who've just gotten reductions? Huh.

C:
My boobs are long enough to fight Sybil's...but they wouldn't win.

Me:
Whatevers. I miss you crazies... Lil Miss Long Boobs.

CF:
Will I see you on April 5th, Sybil?

Me:
Mine are perky & puffy right now. No to April; sorry... crappy

CF:
Crap.

C:
Perky is good. Puffy is tough. What's April?

CF:
T--- board meets in ____ to go over the plans for _____. I'll have to get my budget shit together and present the balances and stuff.

Me:
And they're lubed in Neosporin. Tyca pre-mtg...

CF:
Lubed.

C:

I've thought about a lift, so you'll have to let me know how this goes... It's against my principles, but I look TERRIBLE. I nursed for seven straight years. Ew.

Me:
Yeah, and get this: I can't nip out, but my body tries to! Super not fun!

C:
OUCH

Me:
Lift em! Who cares?!

C:
I'm worried it'll affect the...ahem...feeling. Does it?

CF:
I wouldn't judge you if you did it.

Me:
I already feel more like ME ...

CF:
How long is recovery?

Me:
I feel more sexual, if that's what you mean? I never showed them off to Jan much... as for the nipples, they moved mine, so I may get feeling in them

C:
I'm just worried the erogenous link will be cut. I have enough sexual issues.

Me:
A whole month of doing zip (I have a week left) & then two more months of swelling & no underwire bras...

CF:
Jeez. That's rough. It would be hard to rest and not do stuff.

Me:

My nipples before were sort of dead anyhow... but I didn't like being nude due to their droopy-ness

Yes, hard to rest! I suck at it
I can't believe I'll get to wear pink bras & wear just one sports bra to run in.

CF:
It will be fun shopping for bras now! Millions of choices!

Me:
C, I figure if I'm more confident about them, I'll jump Jan more; this is also why he's excited. No more white, beige, black!

CF:
Dudes like boobs.

Me:
True story.

C:
Dudes are morons.

Me:
So, I'll have new boobies & you'll be in a new country. Wow!
Dudes are dudes...

CF:
I would like to fast forward to August when it's all done with, and I can focus.

Me:
Me too! I mean, for my chest, not so you'll be gone.

CF:
Ha! I'm going to sign off now. I'm hungry and I need to read ____ for tomorrow.

Me:
Bye bye. Love you!

CF:
I'm so glad we chatted!!!!!!! I miss you ladies!!!!!

Me:
Ditto!

C:
ME THREE!

Sushi Barf.

I woke up to Sushi's puking noise. I cleaned up the spray she left behind... then couldn't get back to sleep. I felt my chest, and leftie felt larger than rightie... and the worry set in; empty minds, in the buttcrack of night, do that to ya. Errrg.

I slept on right side, pre-barfing cat, so I thought about curling up on left. I did; it's like how I eat m&ms – gotta equal out the sugar intake on each side. But I got up anyway, checked the chest; it looks smaller than pre-bedtime (leads me to realize that they puff up a bit when I'm too active – went thru a lot of clothing last night), so I put in new padding & came downstairs.

I chatted with CF & C on Facebook last night; C may be heading to a whole other country! This makes me sad & happy for her all at once. I told them I "chopped my boobs off" & that immediately freaked them out about cancer; I need a new way to tell people in a funny manner!!

The less I move, the better.

These are some testy boobies I have.

And, in class right now, I barely did anything... yet it feels like a tumor is growing in leftie. Jeezus. In fact, I'm starting to feel less nerve-based sharp pains – like the phantom balls – and larger phantom-ish tumors that actually cause the area to feel sore & stiff to the touch. Ugh. I had to adjust my bra (another new one from ebay; got two identical to the other one I liked) only once this morning, but the band underneath was uber itchy.

Speaking of bras, so I went through my old BIG ones yesterday in the middle of our "let's got through our shit" spiel upstairs... it's almost tragic that I spent SO much on those things, only to barely wear them or wear them out & get irritated with them on a daily basis. I kept like one really nice one from each size I used to be. Yeah. I hope I don't leap up to the Gs ever again, but I did keep a few pretty 34DDs... yeah.

Now, just minutes after feeling that "OMG, there's a massive muscle tumor about to pop out of my boob" feeling, both are just sore when I touch their sides. Ugh. Oooooofta. I can not wait until I can bend over and not think they are going to pop off. OR, better yet, open up and my pink fat all oozes out onto the floor. Delightfully Demented, I am.

On Pandora: "Let it be." Okay, Beatles. I'll try. First choice: Not to hold a sign at today's rally. Yeah.

March 25, 2013 (Part 3):

Hiding.

I've realized that I hide pain well. I was just talking to Bill, and perhaps he thought I was feeling fine, but really, I'm just uncomfortable – and at times – sore and stiff and dealing with those damn phantom tumor balls!

March 25, 2013 (Part 4):

Me:
On an uber positive note, I think I'm caught up with the grading I kind of "let go" while I was recovering... yay me.

And, in class right now, I barely did anything... yet it feels like a tumor is growing in leftie. Jeezus. In fact, I'm starting to feel less nerve-based sharp pains - like the phantom balls - and larger phantom-ish tumors that actually cause the area to feel sore & stiff to the touch. Ugh.

Now, just minutes after feeling that "OMG, there's a massive muscle tumor about to pop out of my boob" feeling, both are just sore when I touch their sides. Ugh. Ooooofta. I can not wait until I can bend over and not think they are going to pop off. OR, better yet, open up and my pink fat all oozes out onto the floor. Delightfully Demented, I am.

Cheryl:
Loving the visuals here.

Me:
Seriously. In the shower, or anytime before the bra goes on, I think they are going to explode or something. So damn achey. Errrg.

KJ:
No! It will get better!

March 27, 2013:

Googling Boobies.

I've been so distracting with our idiot Governor & the old white guys in Bismarck (okay, some women vote there too – should be MORE of them!) that I have barely noticed any pain lately with my chest. T asked, on the way to the Fargo rally Monday, if I was blogging about both emotional and physical things I'm going through. Then I told her how I googled "natural breasts" and wanted to see what they potentially could end up looking like. Last night, MB said I should check out before/after sites. DUH, man. Been there, done that; a lot of ladies don't really show the final-final result. Like a year or two later type of thing. Just weeks and months into recovery.
Redness & leakage & heat rashes.

I did notice last night (I'm pretty sure it started yesterday) some yellow-ish stuff in the padding from specifically around the areola of both breasts; same thing this morning. And both areolas are reddish in tint and are bumpy. PLUS, yesterday, right before we (Cheryl, KJ) went to the Wilkin, I noticed a heat rash between the breasts. Yay!? No. Errrg. They're already itchy sons of bitches, and then the middle spot had to be too.

I think I took four ibuprophen at the Wilkin yesterday, and that was a precaution since I wanted to stay ahead of any pain from running around all day. The day before I might have used 4-8... yeah. I haven't taken any today. YET.

p.s. Taya also stopped at the big Fargo Walmart for me so I could find more padding. They had TWO boxes! That's it?! Errg. Who else is buying MY padding? Stop.IT.

Tomorrow, I have class, then I'm renewing my damn license (it expired on my birthday in January & I was dying of influenza. No, not dying dying, but yeah) before we hit Fargo for Red Lobster and Menards.

I had a very strange dream last night about the first time he & I would do the sexy sex after my surgery... haven't "gone there" yet, and I thought about asking him about it last night after our conversation about abortion (wtf – I'm great at transitions & foreplay: Honey, if someone rapes me, I'm not having it. But do you wanna do me soon?). Anyhow, in the dream, he was mean to me. I immediately headed out the door before he could say "boobies." He was hollering apologies after me as I huffed my hot ass out of there (wherever "there" was), and saying how great my breasts look, but I was on a mission. Needless to say, I woke up slightly mad at him for no reason. I hate dreams like that. HATE. And, of course, he didn't look like HIM. He looked slightly evil-er than normal. If that's possible. God damn stupid subconscious.

March 28, 2013:

Imagine Dragons.

I don't think I took an ibuprophen yesterday! But I did take a picture of my chest; it's been so itchy – damn heat rash down the middle – and the areolas (as mentioned in the last post?) are leaking this yellow-ish crusty stuff into my padding. I looked online – dangerous, I know – and it sounds like that is normal – called surgeon's office anyhow this morning. It sounds like infections will incorporate, not only a fever, but visual ugliness (for lack of a medical term) and heavier bleeding.

It seems like they go down just a wee bit each night. I feel like I'm basically aggravating them with movement during the day, and then giving them – truly – about 8 hours of healing/rest. That's my perspective on it. I am lubing them up with Neosporin, still, and changing out the padding daily. The nerves spikes and weird tumor-y feelings and phantom balls of pain are almost non-existent (well, for the past few days anyhow – so basically Week 4 is when everything calms the fuck down!?).

And, after a big poop yesterday and two this morning (I know I know TMI), I feel more like me. I am all about the body getting rid of stuff it doesn't use!!!

In the shower this morning, I held them a wee bit, after washing them, and let the warm water pelt my chest because it was so damn itchy. Wish I could've just stood like that all day, but I did bring this ointment with (smells like Ben-Gay)…

Other things to expound upon:

1. No more holding them up… When I used to walk around the bedroom/bathroom without a bra on, I would have to hold them. Right now, they are so swollen (yet perky), that I don't have to. I realize they will sag as I age, but to have smaller ones to start with feels better. And I cannot emphasize how much better my back feels or how straighter I feel just walking!

2. Have one towel & washcloth just for the boobies. One thing I incorporated from the pre-surgery procedure of having to wash myself with that surgical soap was that I used just one towel to dry myself off – a very clean one. Well, I have what I guess you could call a boobie towel & washcloth. They only touch that area, and I wonder if that can kind of aid me in stay infection-free? Maybe it doesn't matter. Never asked.

3. In book, remind women to ask a lot of questions. I had no clue I wasn't going to have drains (she may have said that, but I just blanked out so many things because so much info and feelings were getting pumped into me) or that my stitches would just dissolve.

AND someone said (or I read): The surgery is easy; it's the recovery that sucks. Amen.

March 28, 2013 (Part 2):

Called doc/Erica this morning – played phone tag. I decided to check on that weird yellow stuff that showed up in my padding again (white blood cells mixing with the Neosporin) = it turns out I was ripping the scabbing off (accidentally, really) with the padding = so no more padding!!!

It feels more freeing now to not have that crap bunching up inside the bra.

Happy Four Weeks to Me, yo!

Another bonus: We went to Menards today to pick up lumber and flooring for the third bedroom (and final bedroom/room to complete upstairs!) & I couldn't really help at all. Bummer?! But the boyfriend was all about loading fourteen cases of the flooring himself and unloading it; he thinks he's gained 20 lbs. and I'm pretty sure he hasn't, but whatever.

March 28, 2013 (Part 4):

Me:
Called doc because weird yellow stuff showed up in padding again; it turns out I was ripping the scab off with the padding so no more padding!!!

KJ:
No more padding!

Cheryl:
Unpadded boobies!

March 29, 2013:

No Bra.

Around 7:30 this morning, I got up to pee, and decided to just "unleash the fury" that is my chest. I kept the bra on, but "unbuttoned" it and laid back down for a wee bit. When I decided to get up at 8, I just took it off and walked around the house without it.

Just now, 9am, I put on a clean one after throwing some Neosporin on "the girls" and some anti-itch stuff right under the armpits. I think that the Neosporin might be unnecessary because the incisions are closed up & are pink, but I'm not going to not keep putting that stuff on. I think the extra pinkness and redness around the areolas might be due to the heat rash I can feel coming and going; the redness is in dot form...

Otherwise, this might be the first day that I'd have no problem with him or my sisters seeing them. They look good; they are a little firm and wide, still, but they are starting to look less banged up.

At the bottom, where the T is, of rightie, there seems to be a stitch/suture trying to poke his head through. I want to rip it out, but I don't think that's wise. My instincts are always to demolish things (like blackheads and pimples and scabs around my knees from biffing it, etc.), but I have to force myself to refrain.

So, back downstairs to my brewing coffee to finish the Kathy show & watch the latest Rachel Zoe Project episode, too. The boyfriend said if we both got up before 10:30, we should get BK or McD's. He likes doing that to reward himself for getting up early, I think. So, I've only taken my vitamins (and Biotin) thus far this morning with water. Sometimes, all I need is a little bit of sugar from those gummy vitamins to calm the empty stomach from overnight fasting!

I think the plan for today is low-key. My sis has an interview & then she'll be coming down. We may go through my jewelry and make-up closet? Otherwise, I think the main event is karaoke ("For Jesus") at the Eagles around 9 tonight. Dinner at ma/pa's tomorrow, and then the boyfriend and I will head west to his brother's place on Sunday.

March 30, 2013:

We had a pretty fun time last night, minus some immature girls "from town" who are dumb bitches, ... walked home, even, after karaoke. The sis & I sang "Loser" by Beck; she sang a few with our bro. It was good to chat with our sis-in-law too who "brought" Cubby.

I talked to Shannon, Hil's sis, about my surgery a wee bit. She said I should start using Vitamin E capsules because she doesn't have any scars; I felt a bit of competition from her when she mentioned that – I wonder if others have too. Like, if I have rested longer than she did & I still have scars – that means I suck? But my skin is just different. Obviously. She, along with others previous to this night, said she had no idea I was so large. Yep; I am the queen of minimizers and scarves!

The first thing I said to her was how itchy I was. "You're healing," she said. This is true; why does it take others saying it aloud for me to believe it?

Toward the end of the night, my sis & bellied up to the bar & she said something about beating up K.C.

"I lost my job last week; I'll fucking eat her alive." And in the same tone, I said in a major huff, "And my boobs itch." Ya know, it's enough to be torked about. Dumb people + being uncomfortable = I'll smack someone up.

The agenda for today: shower (sis already did & she's heading to ma&pa's before me/us) with or without my hair getting wet (it's kind of good third-day hair after all the crap I put it in last night) & then head over there for dinner at 4/4:30. After that, I think everyone's heading back to Fgo... and I'll work on some crafty stuff, I suppose, or help the boyfriend paint some things?

March 31, 2013:

I think the boobies are healing OR have heat rash on them OR both...

Looking at pictures taken, they look better yet redder in a few spots (and the redness typically has lil' bumps with it).

Anyhow...

So, my dream last night was about seeing my ex. I think I was at dinner with him & his parents (when his dad was alive), and we ended up kissing in the car ride back to somewhere? Then I ended up with him in a car (or was it current boyfriend?) having to pee & he stopped in this weird spot where a cheetah was hanging out. All I remember thinking in the dream is that if I stayed with current boyfriend, I'd have to tell him I kissed my ex.

Weird! Weird! Weird!

We're heading west to see his bro's family late this morning for an Easter dinner. I hope politics don't get brought up. Or race. Or homosexuality. Ugh. And hopefully, the kids don't try to smack me, or throw stuff, at my chest. His nephews can be a little crazy.

Been thinking about sexism lately. And feminism. My bro & boyfriend said yesterday, about a commercial, that the guy should've gotten a shave from a hot girl in a bikini. And to reverse that & make it less sexist would typically mean a girl would want a naked man to cut her hair... but really feminism is more about not having us look at men & women like "meat" AT ALL. Feminism could be just putting all types of beautiful women in magazines to sell makeup... or to sell tools or to have men selling lotions and cars and cleaning supplies...

BBB

Sideboob #4: Contradictory.

From April 23:

I want to be contradictory; small & powerful. Like my car. Full of ideas, spreading each idea - like a seed - into different topics, into different fertilizer.

I want a small body & large brain. I want to intimidate with my attitude and not just my hair or thighs. This is how I see myself.

Like the best friend to that weirdo bride we saw at the Shout House during our April Girls' Trip; her boyfriend had pipes, she had a size six body that was tight & dressed right, thick hair & kind smile.

It was the first time I think I'd trade bodies with someone (a game I play when I'm bored anywhere where there are a lot of people).

I hope she was a leader. A smart beauty.
Who swears from time to time?

Chapter 9: April 2013. (One Month Post-Op.)

Dermatitus.

The itchiness is normal, but I don't think the lil' red bumps are. I think they are reacting to something. The bra itself? The cream version of Neosporin? I dunno.

As for post-Easter notes: I chatted w/Lacy about my surgery yesterday about it all. On the way home, the boyfriend said that his bro said Lacy was my size... 36DDD... well, here's the thing; she doesn't wear the right size. I can tell because her bras ride up her back, so if she wore the right size then yes we'd be the same.

And he wondered how I knew I wouldn't get that large again. I don't recall being a G when I met him ten years ago, but I was large in different ways; I was wider & like a 38D... and wearing size 18 jeans, too. My body changed as I lost weight, but the weight on top just changed from width to cup; 36DD then 34DDD then 34G or H... I can lose stuff below, but my chest has a mind of its own!

But he's right; my biggest worry is that they'll come back – like they are these evil cousins who are on vacation now. It did take a long time for me to go from a C to a G = IF I was a C in high school? When I was anorexic my first year of college, they were definitely small-ish. But I ate nothing & I think I was a size 10-13 in jeans. When I taught high school four hours later, I dunno what I was. I think I was a D?

Still, in my mind at all those times, I didn't love them. I thought they were large & in the way. When I did "show them off" in that velvet top at Christmas (during grad school?), my mom frowned.

So, he did admit that he's concerned I gain them back & be unhappy. I'm glad he admitted it, yet later he wondered why I didn't eat more last night. I said I can't just eat whatever & keep my weight down. He said that he thinks people can eat whatever if their daily activity is high; I then said that mine isn't right now. And I want to be more active; as the snow – which seems to be sticking around with low temps into April now – melts, I'll be able to safely go on walks, etc. I really want to jog & swim soon, but I know I can't overdo it. Plus, my chest isn't quite pain-free yet; jolting it around would really stink.

I should consider joining Weight Watchers; a new lifestyle of health is 80% what one eats & 20% activity.

April 1, 2013 (Part 2):

Diet/food/lifestyle Sidenote.

-I should go back to keeping a food journal. Can I log into Xanga.com from my phone? = That makes it easier.

-I've noticed lately that I eat when I'm not hungry. Gotta stop doing that; food is everywhere! I can eat whenever! No need to force myself.

-I've noticed that breakfasts don't need to be massive either. I like eating a variety of things at lunch & then heavy protein (with wine, sometimes) at dinner.

-I could try that 8 hour eating someone talked about on The Today Show; fasting 16 hours of a 24hr period... eating from 11-7 for ex; just coffee before that w/my vitamins? Just gotta pay more attention to my stomach & try smaller portions.

If I'm bored = Write or Read to distract myself! Re-read Bethenny's book...? Less pop or no pop & tons of water. More activity of all kinds. More protein & veggies, less sugar!

Remember when I was around 175 a few springs ago? Was that 2010 (the spring we almost bought that other house? Yeah cuz we bought this house in 2011, right?)? I almost fit into my skinny jeans' box stuff! I felt good... should look at those food journals!

April 2, 2013:

Yesterday, Erica got back to me as I was mid-painting the upstairs hallway its first coat of Acapulco Sand... the doc said to just clean up the area as best I could and let it all dry big time before lubing myself up with Neosporin. She didn't say to pad it up or use anti-itch shit. So, this must be normal? As of right now, I'm not itchy, but this morning, I almost came out of my skin wanting to scratch the area in between the breasts. And the righty – where the T meets – has two little yellow/white dots that look like white blood cells holding on for dear life. Good lord.

Just went into the campus bathroom to change the tightness of the bra. I told my officemate how itchy I was, and she said, "I guess this is another thing they don't tell you." Yes, it IS.

So, back to yesterday, I painted the first coat and showered. I let everything dry dry dry, and I even napped, propped up, without a bra on while watching the Twins opener. The boyfriend said a few times that I should just let them be braless for awhile & he offered to do the painting... but I wanted to get active. And after a month of not doing shit, my legs/quads hurt from just painting for an hour. Crazy, right? Right.

After the nap, I went to get groceries, and then took the bra off again. I actually made supper – lasagna cups – without a bra on. Super weird.

April 2, 2013 (Part 2):

Facebook message to my friends just now:

Okay, this is really silly, but I have to tell you all...
Last night, I made supper without a bra on.
It was SO weird. But cool.

The pain is better – still phantom pains here & there, but mostly I'm dealing with major, MAJOR itchiness. Like, I almost ripped them off the other day. But the doc says to continue to cover them in Neosporin. So, whatevers. That's why I didn't wear a bra last night for a bit...

Hope you all had a good Easter break!

I have this small urge to go into the bathroom and unleash the boobies. Just sit and let them "air out." Is that crazy? Probably. But at any point now, since I have finished my grading and classes and meetings for the day, I could go home and unleash them there... I wonder how long it takes for a rash to calm the fuck down? I've had some sort of rash on my chest since last Thursday (I think – didn't I show the breakout to Cheryl & at that point it was just above the breasts in a V-shape: like the ones I used to get from scratching), so I hope by this Thursday, it just vanishes and finds a non-surgery'd person to attack. Yeah.

At home, I think I need to help the boyfriend with the second coat of paint. And then I'd like to work on adjusting some camis to fit me. I bought some nighties – rayon! silk! – a long time ago & was going to use them as tunics or what-have-you, but now I'm thinking I can shorten them & make them into tops for under other tops or blazers or sweaters. Cut off the teeny straps and make larger shoulder straps, etc. THEN AGAIN, for awhile now, for the first year or two after this surgery?? I might be able to wear them sans-bra and be sexy for the boyfriend. Huh. I'll have to see which ones I want to save for that plan. Maybe the pok-a-dotted one since I have a lot of pok-a-dotted tops already? Or I could screw around with all of them and buy a super nice nightie somewhere sometime soon?

Oh, but before hitting home, I should get some goddamn gas. The bug has been beeping at me. So annoying. And I spent $100 at Econo last night, so I got a $.25 off coupon for gas; since it's around $3.50 a gallon, that's a nice deal. Word.

You'd think I was a dude (who just turned into a chick for the day?) with how often I look at my damn tits these days. Jeezus. I'm waiting for a miracle; I'm hoping to open up the bra & suddenly see no redness. Fat chance in hell. It's only been a few days & I'm wimping out, wanting to sit still so they don't ache or itch. Ugh.

Got home & chucked off the bra. Redness & bumps are the same... not worse, but no improvement. A bit of gooey-ness came off the rightie's T area. It looks semi-ugly, and I want to poke at it to get the crevice clean, but I know my skin/body has to do its job. And I have to stay out of its way, too. Super hard. I did itch the in between spot, but not the breasts or incisions... came downstairs braless & tried to distract myself with catalogs from today's mail. Finally lubed them up & put on my least restrictive compression bra. Been putting a bit of padding (a panty liner cut in two) near the T on both breasts. I don't "trust" that area since it's trying to keep three pieces of skin together.

I told the boyfriend I'd do the second coat of paint tomorrow; he said he'd do it tonight... asked if I was feeling crappy & I said I was so itchy. He mentioned taking a bath & maybe I'll shower before bedtime. It hasn't occurred to me that maybe I should be showering everyday; I typically do not (gasp?!). I'm a every-other-day girl (or even every third day – my hair & skin are so dry, as is)... so, I could wrap my hair up & shower the body more. I'll especially do that if this freakin' rash hits the highway quicker.

April 2, 2013 (Part 4):

So, good old WebMD says heat rash is caused by sweating & then trapping the sweat with greasy shit. Um, yeah, so maybe I shouldn't put Neosporin ointment on myself... at all? And instead, if at all, I should use the Neosporin cream? It may plug the pores less? I'll let all the Neosporin I put on after work sink in before I shower & dry 'em & attempt the cream...

As long as I protect the T on rightie, with padding & cream, I should see improvement right?

Last night, I did sit in front of the fan with Neosporin on 'em, and WebMD did mention cooling the skin. This stuff is supposed to go away in 3-4 days!

April 3, 2013:

I thought I had thrown my Neosporin into my bag this morning... turns out, I didn't. And I'd like to put more on that T spot on rightie.

I constantly feel like I am going to fuck up this recovery piece, and end up with an infection and horrible scars. It is a constant worry in the back of my head that I am very annoyed with. I mean, I made it through the first four weeks... and now this last week has been riddled with a heat rash and T spots that look different and NOW today, as in during my 1pm class, I started to feel those phantom twinges of pain again. Full on little blurbs of electricity shooting through rightie (mostly) as I taught and now while I type.

It doesn't help that my period is coming this week (probably within hours) and that the boyfriend jokes about "Well, there goes $30k" every time I reach for something or pick up something a wee bit too heavy. And to add to all of this, that meeting this morning pissed me off (I have IDEAS people) and I'm exhausted from two nights in a row of pretty shitty sleep. Ugh.

I can't wait to get done with my 3pm class, so I can chuck this bra off and put some cream on myself...

April 4, 2013:

It's got to be heat rash, but I may hit the clinic today to pay $25 & have a doc say, "Yes, you are correct. Keep it dry and cool. Go, fight, win!" When it's dry and cool = light pink in color; when it's all warm from after the shower or whatever = redder. Yay. Ugh. Damn fucking skin: just cooperate already!

I thought I had SOME patience; you know, where a kid is crying... and I pick her/him up and say, "I know, I know, the world sucks. It's okay." I have that kind of patience most of the time, but this... this is really testing me, and daily I'm earning a D... maybe a C-.

And the phantom pains come back to visit, too. The "OMG, I have a tumor" in leftie showed up long enough for me to pause mid-conversation with the boyfriend and mumble a swear word. Ya know those weirdos who talk to themselves? I was already on my way towards that, and now these tits are making me talk to my chest. "Settle down, for christ's sake. I'm not even moving."

HIGHLIGHT: I went to Wallyworld last night and bought $150 of shit. Okay, that's not really a highlight, but it made me feel good to buy some cute things like barely-no-support neon-colored sports bras and matching undies. Who doesn't like new undies? I recall that being a major fucking highlight of my immediate post-surgery day; I got to my room and peed and wanted undies on because lube was coming out of me.

Back to Wallyworld... the highlight is that right now, well last night, I fit into a 38C (or was it a D?) front-closure bra. And I'm still swollen! So, at this rate, I could easily be a 36C or 38C or whatever. If I shrink in the cup and band just a wee bit more, I've got the 36C boobies I was hoping for. Yay! And that cotton one I wore for a bit last night really helped the rash; these compression bras are nylon based = that can't be helping the breathing part all that much. Yikes.

Another highlight is that I'm getting my food intake back in check using my other blog to keep a food journal again. I feel better each morning, and I haven't stuff myself stupid since like Monday or Sunday. And besides yesterday's lunch, I haven't had much pop – and even at lunch, I didn't finish the Rootbeer/Diet Coke concoction I created either.

April 4, 2013 (Part 2):

I have an appointment with my regular doctor/nurse practitioner at 1:30pm. Even the appointment lady on the phone seemed concerned for me...

Thus far, I should mention that I have only shown my new "girls" to three people – a surgeon, a nurse, and today, another doc/nurse. Yeah, no normal peeps have seen them, besides me. Is that weird? Maybe, maybe not. How often do people see others' boobs? I'll eventually show the boyfriend, but with how they look right now, he might just be concerned for them and me and not turned on...

I guess that's a fear, too. That he won't be in awe of the newbies. I already came out of the bathroom in a nightie (without a bra), and he seemed distracted with his remodeling work or unimpressed or both... and I think he said, "Aren't you supposed to wear a compression bra?" Yes, but I itch and I want to free the ladies from time to time. Chill out.

I totally have papers to assess (the Ag section handed in their P6s on Tuesday night), but I have no motivation to do so. Like, I almost want to table assessing those things until next week just to semi-torture those students. Then again, they haven't been a horrible class AND if they are banking on the final projects, they SHOULD be worried... and it's not my issue.

So, one of the Ag students emailed me today (we have Friday and Monday left of this damn course) that she wants me to go through all the past projects and explain why she got certain points taken off. I wrote back that maybe she should give me a list; why do they think I should do the work to help them pass?

Ugh. I just want to say, "Look, I have itchy boobs. Come back later. Or never. You earned your grade, and I don't have any patience left." Maybe that's my attitude with the Project 6s, too. "I'd grade 'em, but my boobs itch. So, I'm not gonna. Bite me."

April 6, 2013:

The "no more Neosporin" is working slowly but surely; so, I have a less intense need to itch. Skin is more pink – showed my sis Alisa the boobies this morning & she was impressed with their healing.

Just got back from Fargo a wee bit ago. Fun times. Might have said too much in too blunt of ways, but I can't seem to be timid about my thoughts. But I can't live in a certain way to make others happy or in order to end up in good graces – to compromise who I am to make others feel good?

And... Unfortunately, when I got home & de-bra'd, I saw a tiny spot of blood on rightie's side. Earlier – was it yesterday? (Friday) – I had noticed small bruise-looking spots at the bottom of rightie's areola, but I tried not to worry about it. It may be where the blood came from (or further down that incision). Will keep a watch out on it.

Dad asked how I was. Told him about rash. Ma commented on how small I looked in the tee I made; she wondered if I looked small from the bra, but Alisa corrected her that I was still swollen. She seems to not like shrinkage on any of us; she also put a few unflattering pictures of me from the baby shower online. She seems to do that a lot, but it could be all in my head.

From Thursday's Facebook Message to my friends after the appointment: Contact dermatitis. No more Neosporin; instead, Claritin & hydrocortisone & basic hydrating lotion & cotton bras (or no bra).

First thing she said was, "They look great." And she thinks the incisions are just fine. Thank god.

April 7, 2013:

Remember when Alisa said, after sneezing hard in my bug pre-drinking, that she blew out an ovary? Well, that feeling has followed me throughout recovery. When sneezing, moving myself up in bed, bending over = feels like PLOOP, there goes the boob. Like I'm about to pop something. I'm hoping it's the muscles getting their act together. The doc said all this was normal, but then why not have a handout? Why not say, too, "Oh yeah, you can start running a month out from surgery!" Ugh. I feel lied to sometimes.

And people just appear not to care. Not asking me = I don't care. But that's me. Would I ask a relative how they are? Yes. I think so.

Meanwhile, I'm slightly itchy this morning, but they look pink and a bit smaller... I'm more upset with how much crap I ate yesterday but I did well all week & I'll get on track.

April 7, 2013 (Part 2):

Saw this woman on The Daily Show = COO of Facebook. She wrote a book, Lean In. About making it okay for women to lead. Girls aren't bossy; they are leaders... what we say to boys (onesies: I'm as smart as dad vs. I'm as cute as mom) vs. what we say to girls is crazy. I used to call my niece a weirdo when she was teeny tiny; my sis didn't like this... but if she was a boy?

So, when we think of stereotypes & the surgery I underwent... what are the connections? Did I keep my chest around to make others see me as more sexual than smart? Did I feel more of a sex object with them & that's the underground reason for wanting them gone? I want to be seen as smart & fashionable, but one doesn't downplay the other.

Do I think my boyfriend saw me a certain way with a larger chest? I don't know. I do know that he wouldn't feel like in order to love me, my chest has to be size X BUT THERE ARE MEN LIKE THAT. And women bow to them. He wants me to look Y, so I'll do Y. This needs to be mentioned: my boyfriend right now has not ever said I should be on a diet. I think once he said my chest size was nice because they were "a handful," but he's got large hands. And once he said a gal's belly shouldn't ever be larger than his (the exception was pregnancy).

I think feminism & sexism are connected to this sort of surgery...

April 7, 2013 (Part 3):

Photos.

Downloaded more photos today from camera: I wanted to show off the remodel the boyfriend has been working on in our upstairs hallway... and by doing that, I downloaded more pictures of my boobies. I decided to look at all the pictures I've taken; I am SO GLAD I took a before pic with other recovery shots (that aren't at perfect intervals like week 1 and week 2, etc.) because WOW they look so much better. And the pic I took this morning shows them a tish bit smaller & more circular/tear-drop-ish. So, to those reading who haven't had surgery yet, take a pic the night before surgery!! You'll appreciate seeing the changes.

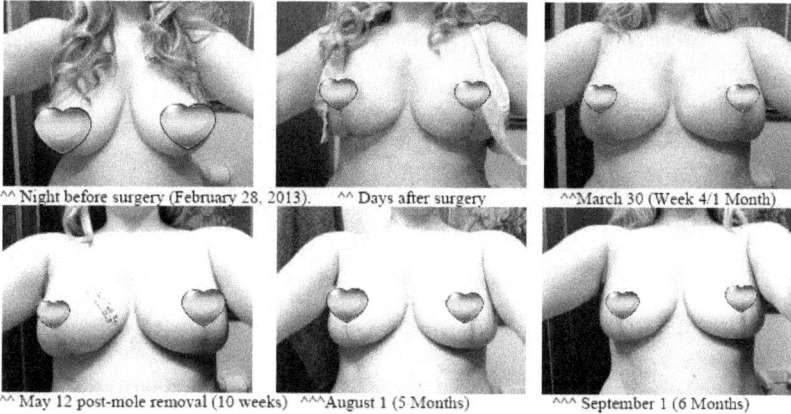

^^ Night before surgery (February 28, 2013).   ^^ Days after surgery   ^^March 30 (Week 4/1 Month)

^^ May 12 post-mole removal (10 weeks)   ^^^August 1 (5 Months)   ^^^ September 1 (6 Months)

BREAST REDUCTION PROGRESSION.

Sidenote: I find myself still referring to my chest as large. Accidentally, then I correct myself, like: "I mean, when they were large," etc. The brain has to catch up.

April 8, 2013:

To the girls via Facebook today:

This might be TMI, but I think my nipples are coming in. The itching & redness has gone down, and yesterday when I downloaded the remodeling pictures, I also downloaded the other boobie pictures I had. It was cool to look at the progress I've made, and they are starting to look less square-ish!

—

Yes, this morning, after showering, I noticed that the nipple part was less flat and more nipple-y. On both breasts! Huh. I'm having strange phantom pains still – mostly in rightie – but it's all bearable.

April 9, 2013:

Maybe, just maybe, Week 6 IS the "lucky number 7 for this whole thing?!?!? The weird stinging twinges are few and far between; every so often, it feels like I'm being pinched (where the incision ends near the armpit on rightie = rightie is an asshole sometimes), but that's about it.

I should almost make a timeline of when what happened, etc. Like when the biggest twinges happened or when I stopped wearing padding, etc. etc.

April 10, 2013:

This is probably not normal, but I find myself wanting to use my boobs as excuses. Like, I used to use grading papers to get out of things. People would be hosting an event, I'd be tired and I'd say, "Oh, so sorry; I have TONS of papers to grade." Yeah. I think the boobies are taking over. Now, a student gets all pissy with me about something, and I want to say, "Yeah yeah yeah. Go away; my boobs hurt." Or how certain people want me to help out with this K-12 conference this summer; some don't ASK me to help, they just assume I would. I want to say, "Um, it's the year of boobs and books. I'll be resting my boobage and writing 17 books. Please leave me alone."

April 11, 2013:

-Got highlights yesterday morning & after realizing that it looked brassy-er than normal, I got some brass reducer shit. Well, halfway into washing it out, I realized I was smooshing my chest against the tub. Damn it.

-Sometimes it feels like I'm growing rocks in them. Remember when you first get boobs? That weird rock feeling? Yeah, that.

-Taking vitamins & Biotin since mid-January = pretty sure my hair has grown an inch. I used to not be able to get it beyond my chest – it would only hit above... now, it curls around the breasts when I bring it forward. Yay.

April 12, 2013:

So, I attempted some sexy time last night by lighting a candle when he was in the shower. But he didn't pick up on the hint, and I'm not going to take it personally. He had just ripped up the carpet in the third bedroom; he was probably exhausted.

We haven't talked much this week; he's been in his own world, and I'm not one to pry because I know – by now – that it won't do much good. He is a chatterbox one week and a mute the next.

I just want to let loose tonight. My hair seems to be getting longer due to the Biotin I'm taking everyday, and I just wrapped up that Ag class (grades in Peoplesoft already, too!!), and I'm writing that textbook, and today marks WEEK 6 of the surgery. WOOT WOOT.

April 14, 2013:

I was right; my sister Robin is pregos again! Yay! I knew it at Easter; sounds like they conceived in Mexico.

And he finally took off his crabby pants at the Dream$ Auction... ugh. We chatted last night about sexytime, but he put it on me again & I guess that's better than him being like, "Let's do it, woman."

We paired up to finish off, almost, the third bedroom yesterday = weekend warriors, like Alisa said before she left. We all hit El Toro for brunch, post-Dreams hangover sleeping. I just put the 2nd coat on while he's sleeping.

Other Stuff: Using Bio Oil (for a few days now) w/lotion on top... they are looking pretty pink & good; they still feel uber solid-y from time to time, like I'm growing tumors, of course!

I guess my ma told her cousin Barb who works at the college w/me; she saw me at Dreams & glanced quickly at them before saying how great I looked. She's a nurse so it wasn't awkward (it can be w/some people – yet I've asked people point-blank what they think).

It's been an easy transition on the outside because I covered them so well before; I'm sure some people are like, "She doesn't look smaller! Why is it such a big deal?" This is why I hope I can shrink the rest of me this summer; I'd love to start the fall tighter & feeling better! I want to start running & swimming!

I do like how perky they are now. And easier to "lock & load" in the morning when getting dressed. Everything fits better, too. I think by my next follow-up, next Tues, I could go for a run or swim??

A Walk to Cool Off.

So, I didn't have to walk to campus today... but it's about 30 degrees out, and this storm we had yesterday is calming the fuck down. It looked like the snow at the end of the driveway was going to be tricky for the bug, so I didn't want to deal with that either. In the long run, I needed the walk. Somewhat for the exercise, but mostly to cool off. The boyfriend kept me up part of the night with his drunk frog legs banging up against me AND to add to that, his snoring that he wakes himself up with constantly. Why can't everyone just curl up in the fetal position and zonk out quietly? Why do I have to be the light sleeper? Damn you Dad and those genes.

Errg.

I got up around 4am or 5am or whatever and went downstairs. The damn cat followed me and insisted on being on top of me, of course. I adore her, but it gets to be too much.

I think I zonked out for about an hour ... from 9-10am maybe. I tried to before that, but it was a no go. Just kept watching the news and the scroll of schools that were closed or two hours late; we weren't one of them, but that's okay because I had canceled my classes due to SKILLSUSA, and that got canceled, too.

Whatevers.

I finally got into the shower around 11am. When I left the house, he was up... doing the trash and looking for his phone charger. I didn't say goodbye. I simply woke up on the wrong side of everything. I'm sure eventually – and this is the pessimist in me – I'll end up having to sleep in a separate bed from him in order to get any sleep. [...]

And that's not even the tip of why I needed to walk to campus to cool off.

I think, in the large scheme of things, knowingly or not, he is pretty much just revving my engines on certain things with no intention of following through. Remember the last time we split for a week? He came to my apt on Loy and said that he'd go running with me blahblahblah. Never happened. The other day I mentioned going for walks together, and he didn't like that idea. Cries wolf a lot. Another ex: When I got the job down here, we celebrated at the Turf, and he said to someone that I was his "ticket out of town" and that we'd get a farm in Fergus with horses. Yeah... that was 2005.

THEN, oh yes there's more, there are all the appointments I made to look at cabins in Fergus because he'd live with me if we had a cabin, and I thought I'd totally commute if I had to commute from a lake. But that didn't pan out, so we looked in town. Nothing was good enough, and I had to pull the trigger (stop the engine from revving and just fucking GO, in other words) on the house we have now. It still took him a few years, and a shitting fishing trip and my surgery, to make him consider moving here. I think he added in, that day we talked, all the, "I'm moving here to start a family" shit to make sure the amount of guilt on me was heavier than the snow we got yesterday.

Men are so bipolar. We aren't. George Carlin was right; we're crazy because they make us so.

On the bright side of things, when I showered this morning, I think it was the first time I didn't guard my breasts from the tough stream. The incision from the areola to the upside-down T was red once I got out, but with a bit of Bio Oil and Vitamin E lotion, they calmed down to pink. I also put some cream-based Neosporin over the top of that = my "problem" areas are where the incision from the bottom of the breast (the upside-down T) to the bottom of the areola; those two T-spots are where I've noticed gaps and had to put more Neosporin.

The rims of the areolas are hard in some spots yet, and there seems to be a suture? It's still along the bottom incision – like a hard foam underwire under my fucking skin – that is keeping them perky. I'll have to ask next Tuesday if that will dissolve or whatever.

I'm starting WEEK 7, kids. I wonder what the two-month mark will bring. And three months may have them at Cs instead of Ds (and maybe my width will go down too; I think I'm around the 38D area).

Random Bits and Pieces.

-Lia Sophia party last night at Shannon D's house. Some know-it-all nurse – who I've never met before – says my phantom tumors are from too much caffeine; well, that'd be great and all, but my SURGEON never said that. AND I don't drink a ton of coffee or pop... I detest know-it-alls.

-Phantom tumors were big yesterday, but I was stressed after that meeting. Diversity Council. I was the only tri-chair for a few minutes, and I was like, "Oh awesome; I gotta run another meeting." I take over meetings because I have to... I will be a leader if need be, but I'm feeling that that gets taken for granted. And the stress shows up in my chest now.

-Just had another phantom feeling when I reached to throw away something. Damn leftie.

"Don't you worry child; heaven's got a plan for you." = I hope someone does. I need to work on my books and nap more.
This weekend will hopefully be a fun getaway. Shopping, girl talk, drinks, yeah...

Week 7.

Lucky #7? We had sex tonight – first time since my surgery – and I showed him the boobies.

He said they looked different & still a bit beat up... I don't know if he realizes how BEAT UP they really were...

And I'm unsure how to take his reaction; if he thought they looked good or bad... I showed him after the sexytime (needed the compression bra on while I was on top – they still feel uncomfortable when I bend over & he made sure not to squeeze me too hard, etc.), & he said that I should've done it before. So, maybe that means they would've – or they do – turned him on more? I dunno, & I am too pooped to care a lot right now.

End thoughts because I need to zonk out: I like them. I am happy with the results; and since they're on ME, my opinion matters 95%.

Girls' Trip Summary:

—I'm unsure why I was there. Did anyone ask me questions? Whitney about my chest at the Loft, yes... I think it was assumed that I was healed & didn't need to be checked on? Dunno.

—Speaking of my chest; it flared up while we were at Shout House. The bass affected the nerves somehow & being bumped by people was annoying & irritating them. Occasional tumor surges sent me to the bathroom to cry it out (& partially have a pity party – I'll be honest); I didn't expect the boobs to do that, and I don't think I should apologize for that.

—I wondered today, while they hit Banana Rep & I hit Old Navy at Albertville, if they were gossiping about me. Saying how crabby I was or how I bring up my chest too much. I don't know, & I don't care. They are achey today & last night, rightie looked a tish bit bruised (small spot by areola) which could've been due to my heavy purse & being bumped.

I have a follow-up appointment tomorrow (9:30); I haven't seen the surgeon & Erica since before Easter (the week after Spring Break)... it's Week 8 on Friday, or officially the Two Month spot. Huh.

I think I'll ask about going swimming... thinking that running might be in the near future, and that biking or walking would be okay right now. I should ask when I'll know I can wear underwire (Month Three mark?) & how else they'll change. Also, I should ask about the hard spots in the breasts, too. Will they dissolve?

Follow-up: talked their ears off*. I almost barfed during breast exam. The sutures will dissolve or not. I can swim & run (be careful). Donating my bras will make me feel better.

My typical routine: I wear a compression bra at night, take off in morning to air 'em out & then shower &/or put on lotion (cream Neosporin, Bio oil, regular lotion-Aveeno)... work on campus in compression bra, come home & switch to sports bra; put on a new batch of lotion/oil on pre-bedtime before putting compression bra back on.

I've been washing bras, in machine but air-drying, after three uses (about).

*I'm all, "and then this nurse said my tumors are from caffeine," "and then my sister said my boobs would get huge again if I had kids," ...

April 25, 2013:

Measurements.
I should've taken measurements in addition to pictures. Yesterday, I measured the chest, and I'm 36″ around the rib cage – under my breasts. The breasts are 41″. So, a difference of 5″ right now; I really wish I knew what the difference was pre-surgery, but I'm sure it was HUGE. Yikes.

Anyhow, if you're reading this (thanks for doing so, by the way) and you haven't had the surgery, please consider photos and measurements. I think I'm still shrinking – it's semi-noticeable every morning. AND last night at stupid fucking Walmart, I bought a red bra. RED. Off the clearance rack for $7... 38D. It's a bit big, but I had to celebrate! The boyfriend was happy when I flashed it at him.

I asked surgeon on Tuesday about many things & her opinion was to not have kiddos passed my early forties. If I want two, if WE want two, I should start worrying about it when I'm mid-37-ish... huh. So, I have time, I said. Yeah.

My appointment started late & then we chatted up so much that I could tell they needed to move onto their 10:30 appt at 11… it's like, ya'll know you talk too much at each person, so plan accordingly. Yes? Eh. I think I brought up that know-it-all nurse ("it's because you drink too much caffeine")… and forgot to ask her if she had any family near Boston during the bombings last week; that would've taken us "over time" for sure.

Double-Time.

So, I hit the 8-week mark yesterday; we toasted to it at Prantes (me, T, Kari H., & B)… anyhow, I gave exercise a whirl today… twice which means I may have overdone it. But the walk at 1-2pm felt new & good; my back/posture felt great; I only had a small twinge when I got home, and it was barely there. The bike ride (7-8pm) was okay, too, once I got air in the tires.

So, yes, this winter-lover went outside on the first nice day of the "spring." I hope this encourages me to continue. I'd like to work up to an early morning workout routine where I do strength-training+maybe some interval cardio (that 4min workout from Youtube or Jillian's 20min workout) before I hit the 3mile loop at run, bike, or walk. I'm guessing all that would take about an hour (more if I walk). OR to even train like I did for cross-country = have a morning workout & a night one?

I just don't want to overdo it quickly; it all has to suit my new chest & it has to be flexible.

Message just now to my gal pals on Facebook:

So… I just put my boobie pictures into a document so I could see my progress. There's definitely progress, but there's also a mole on rightie that got larger in each picture. Like, he's non-existent (looks like a freaking freckle) in my first pic (day or two after surgery), and now he's a full-blown-Hi-I'm-here mole.

I should be a little (or a lot) worried, right? I should have him looked at a.s.a.p (& why not because my deductible is all used up for this year anyhow)!

Thank goodness I took pictures of my dumb chest. Don't know if I would've caught this otherwise.

April 28, 2013:

Walked briskly for an hour today around 1:30pm... Legs are sore-ish & ass feels tighter. Yay. Might do one more long walk before trying to jog 1mile of the 3... or maybe I should just walk for a week w/some strength training & THEN jump into jogging?

*Gotta call doc about mole this week!

April 28, 2013 (Part 2):

Exercise Calorie Counter.
1 hour of leisurely bike riding, at my weight (200), 350-500 calories, depending on speed (high end, 10mph+).

1 hour of moderately fast walking, at my weight, 315 calories, 3mph.

When I start running, 30min of 10min mile pace = 450 calories burned. Less time with bigger burn.

Other = swimming for an hour, treading water, etc. = 350 calories burned.

So, no wonder my legs hurt... I burned almost 700 calories yesterday and then another 300 this afternoon with my walk. Huh. I really like that walk; I have a great playlist, and I am kind of looking forward to it tomorrow morning... starting off my day with exercise and, most of all, meditation and energizing music! I love the daydreaming part of walking, running, and biking. Maybe that's why strength training has never been something I've tried? I have to count reps, watch form, and I can't zone out...

Breast Update: There's a little pink spot, tiny dot, on the incision that goes from leftie's areola to the underside... I put extra Neosporin on it. I don't know if it means anything or if it's just an irritation from daily stuff. YET I'm sitting at the computer right now completely topless. Gotta let this shit dry. But, it's a weird feeling, man. Weird feeling to not have to hold them up. If the sutures never dissolve, I could end up with halfway perky boobies for awhile with little effort! Strangeness.

Sideboob #3:

The Facebook conversation with my friend & former student, MR.

Me:
Hi honey. Did I tell you I'm getting my boobs chopped off tomorrow? Yep. Bye bye back pain! That's the reason for the status; I haven't told everyone (told my boss it was non-life-threatening surgery because his wifey will tell everyone & probably give me the "God loves your body as it is" speech), but yeah... I'm nervous and excited, and I am looking forward to running this summer with like ONE sports bra instead of 17.

MR:
WOW! lol, so this came up on my phone only showing me "Did I tell you I'm getting my boobs chopped off..."! After initial shock, then horror (of course my brain immediately jumps to breast cancer - thank GOD [buddha?] that's not the case!). Then I took your tone into consideration, and I finally decided that since even YOU wouldn't brush something legitimately serious off that lightly, you were probably just doing a reduction - so I'm very thankful that's all it is! Well good for you! I mean, obviously a little bit scary (isn't surgery always?), but alleviating pain is always a good thing. And just think what you can do with the extra money from not having to buy so many sports bras!

Seriously though, thanks for letting me know. And (yes, I know I'm not supposed to start a sentence with 'and') just because I'm paranoid when someone I love goes under the knife, let me know that everything went well afterward, ok? Hope everything goes well!

Me:
But I love starting sentences with conjunctions. I've gotten blasphemous with my sentence structure, I tell ya.

I did have to have a mammogram (super fun! NOT) to check for cancer, but none of that in the system which is good (I have a great aunt who died from it, but no other family history).

For me, it's about my back, my inability to run well with them, my self-esteem when I try on stuff, my "eh" attitude with them because I've never liked them, etc. At my best friend's wedding long ago, I had so much fun, yet when I see the pics (the dresses weren't strapless, but they had teeny straps), I look like the big boobed bridesmaid with straps digging into her shoulders; you could literally see the red marks being left behind. Ew.

So, yeah... I'm ready to be smaller because I'll feel better physically and mentally. Jan's okay with it because he figures I might actually show them off more.

Me:
I will try to get on FB after (surgery is early, and then I stay overnight) to tell people I'm okay.

MR:
lol! I love that I can be a grammar nerd with you, and we both get the jokes other people might not notice. Well since it's basically elective AND for your own health, I'm all for it! And (there I go again) thanks ahead of time!

March 1.

Me:
Hey hun- it went well; not in too much pain. Jan says I'm moving my arms too much; he's here with me. Doc said it went better than most!

MR:
Well good! That's the report I wanted to hear! And really, isn't Jan just pretty stoic anyway and not given to grandiose gesticulation (alliteration ftw!) like some of us are? So clearly he just doesn't understand. Thanks for keeping me updated!

March 4.

Me:

Update: Saw boobies for the first time yesterday in order to change the padding between the compression bra & skin. They are smooshed... looks like they got into a boobie fight with some other boobs and lost. Don't know if I want Jan to see them; they are not pretty, but I know they'll change.

I could've showered yesterday, according to the doc, so I will today. Will attempt to have Jan do my hair or I may go down to the salon in town.

Pain is okay = the nerves cause twinges every so often that really suck, but that means they are trying to get their act together. I'm already down to just one hydrocodone very four hours; using ibuprophen for the headaches BUT NO BACK ACHES! Woot woot. I've been resting a lot & pretending to "be a T-Rex" as the doc put it. My arms don't hurt, but I can't overextend them until everything is healed up.

I can't wait to sleep on my sides & poop! TMI?? Keep me posted on what's happening with you; it'll make me feel better to be connected to stuff outside the house!

MR:
YAY for no more backaches!!! I don't even have boobs, and I get those sometimes. Although, what are the headaches from? Getting woozy because you're not as solidly planted to the ground? |
Once the bruising goes down, and the blood vessels and nerves figure out what the new status quo is, I'm sure they'll look less abused.

I love the mental image of being a T-Rex; mostly because I can totally see you doing it (not to mention Al, Robbie, and Jeddicus too!).

Sleep on your sides wasn't TMI - pooping would be from anyone else, but from you it just seems like normal conversation.
Not too much going on with me. Still going to Physical Therapy twice a week (Tuesday and Friday) up in Shoreview, which is actually pretty fun; I've been going up there for almost 3 years now, so I know everyone pretty well, and have come to know several of the other patients as well.

Loft is still in the process of being renovated. Of course I keep coming up with new ideas too! Which totally doesn't help, lol. OOH, and when my folks were down last week for an ophthalmology appt, my dad (the pretty straight-laced, buttoned down, semi-conservative [although now voting Democrat - wisely ;)] Radiologist, turns to me and asks "Have you ever considered selling paintings?" I was floored! I mean, I love the idea, but I guess I'd never thought I was good enough to actually SELL my work. So that might be my new adventure!

Ok, now I've talked your ear off (typed your eyes out?), but I think that's about all the "news" I have! Hope it helps!

Me:
I loved ALL those stories! So fun! And the painting thing sounds uber cool. We have a new art gallery here in town & there are some inspiring local artists there... I just donated money there to keep it all going.

I hope your body & mind continue to heal along with mine!

MR:
Thanks, and ditto!

March 11

Me:
The boobies ache less if I move less. They are extremely sore bitches.

MR:
Ohhh! (But also "lol"!) Can you be sedentary for a little while?

Me:
You sound like Jan. I don't "do" this "be dependent on others" thing well. He just told me tonight, "If a doctor told me to do nothing for two weeks, I would use that to my full advantage."

MR:
Hahahaha, Lord knows that's what I would do! I'm with you though - can you imagine what it was like being in the hospital for as long as I was?!

March 12

Me:
You win the Patience Award! I'm so antsy... and I started grading
stuff yesterday; he said, "The grading will be there when you go
back; you have one whole week to relax & do nothing." I didn't tell
him he's right, but...

I finally got a fairly good night's rest. Sleeping on my back is okay
some of the time, but I can't wait to sleep on my side.

Were you able to sleep well in the hospital?

MR:
LOL, you and I both know that is one award (among many!) that I
will NEVER win! I can see how grading might almost be therapeutic
for you right now, a sense of some normalcy and all. I'm glad you got
some sleep! I really don't remember what sleeping was like for me in
the hospital - which tells me either it was probably fine, or I've
blocked it out! I'm thinking it was probably fine though? There were
people in and out of my room almost constantly, but I think between
life in NYC (which was just plain noisy) and being just exhausted
while I was in the hospital I probably tuned it out. When do you go
back to work?

Me:
We're on Spring Break (reason I did the surgery when I did; I only
have to use one week of sick leave), so next Monday is the first day
back. I tied up any loose ends on Feb. 28, so I only have some
grading to catch up on (and I don't have to grade every tiny
assignment I gave to my f2f classes, really) ... yet Monday's my
busiest day (3 classes & 2 meetings). It'll be weird to make sure I
don't carry 10+ pounds of anything or raise my arms up too high.

Chapter 10: May 2013. (Two Months Post-Op.)

Exercise: Walked & biked Sat; walked Sunday; walked Tuesday; walked/ran this morning at Blikre (too damn cold – was cold Wed morning too & on Monday morning, I needed the sleep!)... trying to do three miles under 60minutes. I did double-up on bras for today's exercise, but not because I needed it really... it just feels more secure that way? Might be a hard habit to break.

Routine: Before the day begins & pre-bedtime = Neosporin cream rubbed in, then bio oil, then some sort of vitamin E lotion (Aveeno or Udderly Smooth – found at Walmart – or Fruit of the Earth Vitamin E skin cream).

Small pink spot on leftie: I finally put some ointment on that weird spot (think I mentioned it in a previous post) and then covered it with a bandaid. I had picked at it, and the white stuff was the healing juice our body makes, I think. So, I won't be touching it again. It seems to do well with the ointment and coverage.

Mole: Haven't called a derm about it yet.

Notes:
—I love only worrying about wearing one of like three bras that fit just fine.

—Had a few twinges today after putting on a new sports bra; I dunno if it's the bra or my activity this morning (ran at 12 minute mile pace for five min – sounds slow, but I am right now).

Other:

—Hil is at hospital with preeclampsia; baby could be born tomorrow! On her birthday!

—Lunch today with Megan & lunch tomorrow with department before Math Olympics; I'm the Number Fairy!

Pink and Blue Spots.

Blue spot first: I'm an auntie again! Jilary had a boy yesterday on Hil's bday; his name is Emmett & he's 6lbs8oz & 19 3/4"... what a cute peanut who looks like his daddy!! We got to see him today, and now I'm beat from that trip & Math Olympics last night!

Ooooooofta. The boyfriend went up last night to deal with spring cleanup week (putting out leftover junk from his place there)...

Pink spot: The spot on leftie I mentioned last Sunday hasn't gone away. I did pick at it and then put bandaids on it this week w/Neosporin. It looks like dermatitis again; it's reddish & bumpy, so no Neosporin for a day or two I think. I should make an appointment for this week = with a dermatologist for that mole.

Exercise: I haven't done much since Thursday, but I'll try to get a walk & maybe a bike ride in tomorrow since I'm beat today, & it's raining.

OMG.
It's here.
The last week of the school year.

And this year... well, it was not easy. September and October seemed like years by themselves, a colleague who retired might not be replaced, and I decided to chop up my body before Spring Break.

If this was Year 8, and I have 20+ more to go, I guess I should just hunker down and enjoy it all. With a drink in my hand, of course.

I don't think I have much BOOB news today. The redness around leftie is disappearing little by little; I haven't put on even lotion today. I did go onto HSN.com and get these AH-HA bras that I've heard some things about. Ordered two packages of different kinds, so we'll see.

*I did go for a walk "this morning" (more like 12:30pm – slept in until like 10am) & plan to walk tomorrow morning, too. However, all the running around I did on Friday should count towards something... I think my goals right now, exercise-wise, are to do 3 miles of something three times a week with some strength-training in there even if it's all squats and abs.

May 6, 2013:

I took a pic this morning. My chest felt sore when I got up, & I've noticed that when they wake up that way, they've typically shrunk a wee bit. Leftie's pink spot is getting better. I'm going in to see a dermatologist Thursday morning (9am, Fargo). I might just stay overnight w/Alisa, so I can shop & see Emmett!

May 10, 2013:

I've got WAY too much going on with my chest. Not bad things, but too many things.

1. The suspicious mole that has shown up since the surgery was deemed by the Russian dermatologist as nothing. My sister joked she might send me home to "rub some vodka on it" (said in a Russian accent, of course), but instead she shaved that sucker off and now for a week I have to put Vaseline on it with a bandaid. Longer if I want absolutely no scar.

It's all about scars, isn't it? Sounds too simple, but really. Isn't life all about scars? Which ones stick around, which ones are hidden, etc. Yeah. I've had five Grey Goose cranberries, so I'm a philosopher, kids.

2. The Russian tells me the red spots on my chest – I felt they were heat rash related – are acne spots. Oh yay, I think. Now I have to add another weird fucking ointment to my daily routine. Fuck you acne.

3. I can now bend over and tie my shoes without shit getting in the way. I noticed this while chucking on my fake Chucks in my sister's Honda; she said, "Yay for you!" It's weird that teeny tiny things are different. Like, after Commencement tonight, we hit up Prantes & goofed around – yes, a chemist, a few Englishers, a micro-biologist, a state trooper, a chemical engineer, and a librarian. At one point, we ladies did the boob shimmy, and my chest does not move side to side as it once did. This makes me happier than it does sadden me. On to smaller and better things, I suppose!

4. I'm still coating the boobies with Bio Oil or Vitamin E oil before bed and in the morning, before adding lotion (Aveeno or that Udder stuff). Adding to that, of course, the acne routine and covering up the damn mole. Jeezus H Christ, chest, let's get things figured out already. Good lord.

5. I also took measurements this morning. There is still no change from the 36" around the bottom and 41" around the mid-breast area. Huh. But it's not even three months yet, so I should just calm my horses. In fact, today is Emmett's one week birthday and my... um... damn I detest math sometimes... 10 week anniversary of being chopped up.

May 13, 2013:

I am itchy (AGAIN!) from this damn bandaid I have to wear over the mole hole. It's leaving a bandaid mark, too, which is uber fun times! Ugh. Damn fucking chest. THEN the other day – yesterday – I noticed that rightie looks larger-ish in the progress pic I took. Here's a good question = How do I know what bumps in the boobies are common & which ones are worrisome? None of them? I'm leaning that way, but there is a lump-ish thing at the top of rightie's areola (have I mentioned this already? feel like I have), and it's not mimicked in leftie.

AND those three acne-ish spots need CONSTANT cream on them. I thought they were heading out of town, but then bam – I went for a sweaty walk yesterday, and they are back to say, "Hi." Little fuckers.

Anyhow... the boobies both felt sore-ish this morning (I'm all about the ISH today, eh?), and so once again, they did look a tad bit smaller. I need to be less focused on the day-to-day looks of them, I suppose, and more on the week to week stuff. Like with weight loss = you won't see differences daily. Duh. I just want them to shrink a bit more and get more tear-drop shaped, ya know. I'm not even to Month 3 yet, and I'm wanting bigger results. Sheesh.

THE REST OF THIS WEEK sees me doing one more Marketplace for Kids event (it's tomorrow, and it's without anyone who has drama, so YAY for me!) and then possibly helping out Jilary after baking for some ADK-ish event Thursday night. I might make my slutty cupcakes? Dunno. Oh, and I think I could go to sand volleyball tomorrow night... and the Faculty Fishing Trip is Wed (although the boyfriend fished that lake this weekend and scored nothing, so we might bypass that event). So, yeah, Thursday is quiet except for The Office finale. Friday through the weekend = nothing planned yet; I do know that it's the Fargo Marathon, though.

May 17, 2013:

Okay – My body. So, leftie still has rocks growing in it. The rocks move about. The hardness above rightie's areola seems to have disappeared, but NOW where the "mole" was removed, I have itchiness from the sticky bandaid shit. ERrrrrg. At least they feel like they are shrinking and at least they are perky.

I have to poo now.

May 18, 2013:

Backstory: Yesterday, I got home around 9pm. I didn't say Hi when I got in. I didn't kiss him goodnight, either, but he had a cold sore & came up to say goodnight while I was topless – drying my chest's oil & lotion. Don't know if he was even turned on by them.

May 20, 2013:

I noticed a weird pain in rightie yesterday & had a sharp one for five sec in leftie today. I'm still going through growing pains. Yay?! Ugh.

In other health-like news, I'm trying out these HCG drops. I heard about the "diet" via Pinterest & found cheap drops online. A person is supposed to start the drops pre-eating three times a day: days 1-2 are when you should pig out on fat-filled crap... days 3-21 or 40 are lower calorie days (somewhere between 500-800). Someone online said she just lowered her caloric intake with these drops and saw changes. I'm going to give it a whirl. I barely ate much Fri & Sat (partially due to our "discussion" on Wed), and I felt okay & my tummy looked smaller Sun morning.

I haven't even told the boyfriend about the drops – probably means I don't have faith in it & know it's a crock. Or just unhealthy. But I figure I need to lower my intake anyhow (and eat more protein, smaller portions), so if these goofy drops help = yay!!

Yeah. It's my last meal to "pig out" (harder than it sounds)...

Need to bike or walk soon (been rainy!); they say light exercise is okay on these drops. I need more strength training anyhow!

Last thing about boobs: I need to cherish that even though no one thinks I'm smaller, I FEEL so great. And it's nice to wear very little to support them right now. Awesome sauce!

Moore, Oklahoma saw a big tornado today = Morgan (Jan's sister-in-law) is okay as is their house.

May 23, 2013:

Today: I bought veggies & seeds (rhubarb batch $15; everything else at Emery's = $35) & saw Kitri at Wallymart. I told her "thanks" for sharing her breast reduction story last summer with me.

Tomorrow: We get black dirt delivered. Then, we'll hoe the granite box & plant new stuff (more perennials); plant rhubarb batch, then have drinks with Taya & my sis.

Saturday: Garden some more? Visit w/Audrey?

I joined an online breast reduction discussion group on Real Self? Asked about sizes at month 3, etc.

Note: Using vitamin E oil has helped my facial skin, too; I add oil to my under eyes when I put it on the boobies.

Mini-Updates:
— Gave up on HCG drops last week.
— Got a letter from boyfriend's dad Friday; he has cancer. His mom had a crummy week with her hubby finding that out, her daughter being near a bridge collapse (Sonja- Seattle), her daughter-in-law being in the middle of a tornado (Moore, OK)... and her sister having stage 2 breast cancer instead of 1. Sheesh.

— He, the boyfriend, went with his bro and nephews to Mora today (return tomorrow); they wanted to see their dad and get a cow.

— I have gone onto a forum about breast reductions recently and started my own profile. It seems like truly EVERYONE's experiences are different AND yet the same. And many, MANY want to be smaller than what their plastic surgeons say. A few didn't get to the C/D range they even wanted, and some gained weight (hypertrophy) anyhow... (happens if the surgery is pre-20s or if a woman gets pregos and doesn't lose the weight). So, my fears are concurred and yet it's nice to be able to go onto that forum and read others' experiences. A few are keeping side blogs, too, like I am. I don't know if many have thought about creating a book from the experience, but oh well. Maybe some aren't readers and didn't look on Amazon like I did only to find cancer-related stuff.

— As of right now, I am semi-sore after workouts or even gardening, and I do feel some twinges in the armpit area. I am still coating them in the mornings and at night with oil and then lotion. The mole area is healing well, and one thing I did notice via the forum pictures is that my surgeon did a great job of stitching me up well. Many ladies had stitches burst and crap like that. Ew. I just had dermatitis and a stupid mole. I may have lucked out thus far? Who knows, but my incisions are not raised and they are pink.

— Anything else: Well, I know that I HAVE to do something this summer = exercise and diet-wise = IF I want to return to campus in the fall with a new body. I know I can do it, too, and if just lowering my portions and biking twice a day is what it'll take, then let's get on board! I am sore from gardening the other day, and I like that feeling. I'm semi-hungry now, but that's okay. I should go to bed semi-hungry! [What did I eat today? Cereal, coffee, protein-based cereal bar, almond bark for breakfast; pizza for lunch; cookie dough yogurt for snack after a nap and then potatoes and corn for dinner...]

May 27, 2013 (Part 2):

Dog Ears.

Sidenote: I forgot to mention that I learned on the forum (realself.com) that I have dog ears = where the incisions make a little blurb of skin on the sides. Huh. I have the most noticeable one on the inside of rightie...

Other Boob Stuff: I had purchased an Under Armour sports bra with the girls on our girls' trip (4/20) without trying it on. It is a Large, and was too tight. Today, I wore it almost all day; it fit just fine. Yay! Then I put on these size 38 cotton bras (from Wallyworld; three for $9), and they felt too big, so I bought 36s out there today. I thought about getting more wireless bras like the red one I scored out there (wasn't that one a 38D?), but even though the 38C looked plenty big, I decided to wait. I might try to hit Kohls on the way home from Valley City on Wednesday. I like that place – not Victoria's Secret – for bra selection!

May 27, 2013 (Part 3):

Another Facebook conversation:

Hi all =
Just had to share a happy update about my freakin' chest. I bought an Under Armour sports bra in the cities in April. It's a size Large, and I totally thought it would fit, but it didn't then. HOWEVER, I just wore it all day today, and it was a perfect fit. So, I'm shrinking little bit by little bit.

I joined an online forum for this sort of surgery recently, too. It's interesting to read VERY similar fears and concerns = that we won't be the size we want to be (so many larger ladies want to just be a damn C!) & that we'll gain the boobies back overnight in some freakish way.

I hope you all had a great weekend. Jan headed to Mora with his brother to check in on their dad; we found out Friday that Art has prostate cancer (they'll know more tomorrow as far as what stage he's in, etc.). I'm not super worried for him yet because he's a tough guy... and I get this feeling they caught it early.

Yeah...

I'll end on a good note = Wade texted us this weekend that he was finally given the GREEN light to hire a newbie! He said he'd tell me/us more this week.

Check you all laters!! -S

May 30, 2013:

I couldn't sleep last night, right away, and I was thinking of him & us... so I went to talk to him in the garage. He said he's keeping things to himself. He's said that before... yet he did say that he's trying to figure things out.

Huh.

Oh, yay... I woke up to my period today. I'm exhausted. I need a day to do nothing, perhaps? BUT it is Alisa's birthday!

*Looking back through blog entries; did I have a downer feeling at the start of last summer? Dunno, but when we were living apart, things were rocky-er. Huh.

Chapter 11: June 2013 (Three Months Post-Op).

—Measurements: Almost at 35" around rib cage & 40" around breasts!

—Remember the fears I had about buying the house, two years ago? I love our casa. I think the first time I felt "cool" about the house was getting dropped off by a cab awhile back – and I though, "Yeah, this is my BIG HOUSE, suckers."

—The boyfriend had to remind me of the house anniversary last night. I was highly intoxicated. It was cute that he remembered.

—MB, the other day at Cheryl's (Saturday?) = "How are the jugs?" I laughed. Then he said, "No, for real. How are they?" And I gave him an update. He's a good hubby & friend.

—The boyfriend's parents (and youngest sis) came by yesterday and today. We ate a lot (the boyfriend used the Holland grill to make quite the feast!), talked a lot, and took them a tiny tour of our town via the boyfriend's "new" truck. I am worried about his dad – has prostate cancer – but he looks good & seems not too stressed about it. There will be a bone scan next week (?) and then his surgery soon after to take the whole damn thing OUT. I hope the bone scan shows that it stayed put in his prostate & didn't venture elsewhere.

—I just read a blog entry, via Pinterest, about a woman (tiny woman at 5'6" and 130lbs) who lost 13lbs in two weeks. The food/eating/diet was very paleo = baked or grilled meats and veggies; the exercise was mostly strength-training (using a kettle ball mostly) with intense cardio in the middle. I'm thinking I'll use her exercise list to start (using a lighter kettle ball; she used 15+ pound ones and mine is 10, I think) and throw in bike rides here and there. My eating needs to tone itself down a bit, too, on the sugar side of things. I shouldn't have purchased ice cream yesterday when we got groceries; I'm too tempted by it, and if I let it sit, I'll be upset that it went to waste money-wise. Ugh.

Oddly enough, I know that strength-training will affect my cardio-loving body the most. And it takes less time, really. The video along with the blog was less than 15min. Then again, the girl doing the video was in shape, so it could take me longer. But I figure if I do that 15+ min strength-training every morning and then go for a walk or bike ride later in the day (plus, eat smaller portions and less sugar and more water)... that I could see results. I think just doing strength-training could lead to results, too, but I'm bigger and need the cardio to burn off existing fat = she was building up muscles to burn off fat mostly and probably didn't need the extra calories burned??

Anyhow...

-The chest is looking good. The mole scar, and the incisions, are slowly fading. I think I am due for a progress photo soon. I was a bit sore this morning, so I did take five ibuprophen before we did stuff outside.

Short-Term Goals:

—Physical: This week, I would like to bring strength-training into my exercise routine and keep the bike rides & walks going... also, from tomorrow onward, I want to only eat when I am really hungry. I want to drink more water, eat protein-based dinners, and go to bed a little hungry.

—Intellectual: Get the fall class "remodel" completed, so I can get paid for that!!

—Spiritual: Start reading at least one book that is from the campus library and has been renewed a million times!

—Joined a Facebook group related to health yesterday; a secret society, kind of.) And the evil in me thinks, as I watch & read other posts: "Please don't go 'on' diets – this should be a lifestyle change; reason I'm not giving up liquor." & "5Ks are nothing, really." Etc. Etc. I'm a judgmental bitch!

—Did a kettle bell exercise yesterday morning; was sore by sand volleyball time! Called them kettleballs on Facebook! Ooopsie.

—Weight taken this morning, post-mini-workout, pre-breakfast: 200lbs. I took pictures of what will hopefully end up as "before" pictures, too, in my compression bra/basic black biking shorts.

—Already turned off the notifications for that FB group I joined. Ooofta. Everyone's gotta talk about running, running, running. Been there, done that, and postman's syndrome ain't no fun. You'll burn calories, but your body won't change as much unless you incorporate strength-training or intervals of that cardio. Whatever.

—I took weight and pictures Wednesday (I think that'll be my weigh-in day? I think I wrote about this in a previous post), and I've done kettle bell workouts for two days & today was a pretty tough bike ride. IF I had to give myself a goal, I'd like to get down to 175 by the time school starts up again. I think that's do-able. Isn't that about 2lbs a week? Maybe it's more? 12ish weeks …

—Food: I had a pretty low calorie count yesterday before I went to Cheryl's to help decorate. I snacked out there on light margaritas and kettle corn popcorn and chips/salsa. I don't think I ate anything when I got home. Today, I had sausage/cheese/egg/hashbrown skillet for breakfast & coffee; cookie dough Greek yogurt for lunch; apple for a snack after my bike ride; tortillas w/cheese & then cereal for dinner. I think I can mostly keep my meals to 300 calories… then I have leftover calories I can throw at drinks every so often. If I really, really listen to my stomach, I don't need that much!

-The boyfriend did ask how summer school was starting up on Tuesday, and yesterday he asked if they fed me and gave me drinks at Cheryl's. Looking back, this has been the first non-talkative day for him. Oh, and yesterday, he made me a new deck table!! Out of scraps!

—I dislike summertime. I think I've written about this before, but it doesn't occur to me how much I like routine (and having to be somewhere, for a class or a meeting) until it's effen June. Sure, those weeks after graduation when I'm de-stressing and napping and sleeping in is nice, but then I need stuff to do. Granted, I DO have stuff to do, but I've already taken care of one deadline (July ?: Remodel all of fall's Eng120 with new edition material)... and the online students won't need me to email them until Monday... their first assignments are due next Sat (June 15). Yeah. So, I have the textbook – the anti-textbook – staring me in the face. I guess I could rework Eng110 and World Lit, too... yeah. And there's one student with an Incomplete; I should review his shit. AND our interview committee won't happen until the end of June.

—TO ADD to that paragraph, the boyfriend is around a LOT more this summer. He's not working (yet?), and I think he wanted to go fishing today-tomorrow evening in South Dakota but that fell through. Last summer, he was here enough. We must do better – attitude wise and sex wise – when we have to be apart. Absence makes the heart grown fonder. And gives us tons more alone time. I was looking forward to, kind of, having tonight and today and tomorrow to myself. Honestly.

—Anyhow, I'm letting him do whatever and not trying to bug him too much. I could bother him with my wacky-ness, but I'm pooped out and if me ignoring him will help both of us (with the alone time thing), then yay!

—We have nothing going on tomorrow, but Saturday is one of my pieces (pretend nieces) graduation party; we then will hit West Fargo for my nephew's baptism. Kind of a busy weekend, I guess, followed by another week of nothing and a weekend of my grandparents' 60th wedding anniversary party in the cities (June 15). Yeppers.

June 9, 2013:

—That FB group: water water water... blah blah blah & they all run but have regular bodies, as in, no definition, really. I want muscles! Don't they want muscles!? Yeah!

—The picture of me with siblings at the baptism: my chest is small, but I look thick around the middle. It could've been the layers of dress/tee w/not standing up straight... room for improvement.

June 10, 2013:

Well, this morning, they looked like they were starting to "drop" a bit. I still have hard spots along the underside of the breasts, though. The sutures are hanging tight.

I have too many things going on in my head right now. I worked out with the kettle bells around 7:30-8 this morning before having a pretty healthy breakfast. Now, I'm trying to decide whether to go to Fergus to shop or just shop in town for a dress (could hit thrift store, that secondhand shop by Mother's Hubbard and the one in between with the weird t-shirts... plus JCP)... yeah, the two dresses I have – the maxi from Old Navy & the Eileen Fisher bright yellow one – aren't enough options for Gma/Gpa's Anniversary party this weekend. I guess I need more. WHICH is why I am also on ASOS.com saving things to purchase. Sheesh. But they DO have gorgeous dresses; I've kept two skater types – that black one with flowers and the one with pink kisses on it. Good stuff.

And I have my online class to worry about – will email them tomorrow with that letter I always send out. I also have an Incomplete to wrap up. AND I think I need more anti-textbook stuff off my office computer. I should either nap and then bike around to the office and downtown to shop or do those things and then come home to nap... I think I zonked out around 2am, but woke up at least twice before just getting up at 7:30am. That's not enough rest!!!

So, yeah... too much going on.

Oh, and I saw a way to make DIY candles on Pinterest, too. They would make cool gifts for the grandparents and my godmother (her birthday is this Wed?)...

June 10, 2013 (Part 2):

— Chest seemed to look like it was drooping, but the picture I just took [didn't] show a major change. It's all in my fucking head at this point, eh?

— Don't tell anyone, but this FitnessPal on my iPad/iPhone is definitely nice for figuring out calories in and calories out. It has me at only 1200 a day which I think is low, but whatever. Some site I looked at figured I was burning 2000-2200 just by breathing each day.) I am not a small girl, but I might turn into one.

June 10, 2013 (Part 3):

— Doubled-up on workouts today because I was bored. Sheesh.

— So, I appreciate that I can read him. And I appreciate that we argue fairly well; we haven't had any major blowouts or whatever, but when he gets testy, it's tough to know how to navigate.

— He got upset that my ex had seen me in my undies when we talked about weight last night (told him the story about Jason saying I had hail damage on my ass); I was like, "Honey, that was three years before you and like 15 years AGO!" Jealousy does reside in him sometimes.

June 12, 2013:

— Down 2 or more pounds from last Wed (198??). Well, at least, the non-digital scale of mine wasn't at 200 this time...but not at 195 either. Dumb thing. So, considering that I didn't do super well eating-wise this weekend, that's reassuring! Keep up the healthy!

Sidenote: I am sore still today... after doubling up on workouts Mon, I shopped & biked everywhere yesterday (dinner was vodka, cranberry, & seeds... should try club soda instead?), so I think my body needs a low-key day or good food & rest. Egg white & cheese muffin for brkfst? Walleye for lunch? Yeah.

Found myself sleeping ON my chest last night. Yikes. Hope that didn't do too much damage! Been trying to just sleep on my sides...

June 14, 2013:

So, this week, we had a tiff over his job searching & money worries, etc. we didn't talk much for a day or so... then, I asked "what the hell is going on?" yesterday evening. He says he doesn't want to go down to the cities this weekend.

I blew a gasket. I spewed out everything I've been pissed about & then stormed out to call my sister Alisa then my brother Jed to see if I could drive with them. Only Jed picked up. THEN I just couldn't be in the house anymore, so I went for a bike ride. My typical route (was my third workout after kettle bells & gardening)... got home & talked w/Alisa. THEN he changes his fucking mind & we get Twins tickets.

Oh.My.God.!!!!!

June 17, 2013:

What a rush of a weekend. The party Saturday went by quickly – we were there for like 4 hours, and it poured on us at the beginning. I talked mostly to my family and then Kelcie, Bean, Jessica... we took a cousin pic and that was insane. My tunic dress, from ASOS, was too roomy, so I look a little big in the photos, but I don't care. I got to wear a tiny sports bra, and that's it! I showed off my upper arms, too!

Then we hit the hotel to swim and chat in Jilary's room. That's always fun times; Jan & I hit the Mediterranean pub across the street after for pizza and drinks and baba ganoosh (spelling?), etc.

Just as we got home, on Hwy 210, he brings up the job stuff again and how to get a Master's, and he said he didn't know he could get a Master's online, etc. We kept chatting about it all the way to the house and unpacked a bit... at one point, he said that he had given up on the kids talk we'd had. I don't know what that means, but once again, it must not be something he wants to fight for? He likes to put things "in my court" that don't belong there. Him deciding to marry me or get a job or get more education or whatever are not only my calls to make. He doesn't like making decisions – gets buyer's remorse. Hell, he hasn't decided anything, beyond what truck to buy or what boat to buy or what lake to fish on for 10+ years. I guess I've only decided on a job and a house, but those seem like larger decisions to me!

Anyhow... I am wiped out physically and mentally from this weekend. I'm sore somehow (did swim on Sat night and then walked a lot yesterday when I wasn't in a sauna of sun), so I might take it easy with a walk or bike ride today.

And the hoops for my boobies continue! Ugh. This better be the third and final issue with them!? Right?

Facebook messages to Cheryl & KJ:
OH, and p.s. I have to go to the doc again for another rash. This time, it started just on leftie's areola... well, I've tried a few things (not putting Neosporin on it, just lotion or vitamin E oil, no lotion or oil) and it's not going away. AND rightie is starting to show signs of it. UGH.

Update on clinic visit: Good news is I sweat too much, bad news is that it caused a yeast/fungal infection on my boobies. I was given a prescription for some ointment & told to stop lubing them up so much. Who knew you could over-moisturize!? I think I'll try to wear my compression bras less; they trap moisture. At the Twins game yesterday, I was a sauna, so I'm sure that didn't help my situation. Sheesh.

Cheryl:
Poor little boobies!

KJ:
So the message was to quit taking care of yourself? Just kidding but I do have more lubing and frequent rubbing comments.

Cheryl:
I avoided those, they would be pretty fun though... Sybil, the excessive boobie lube and all that jazz!

Me:
I know. I've been taking care of them TOO well? And exercising! I knew I sweat too much, but good lord. Gave myself contact dermatitis and now a yeast infection on my chest. Go ME! I told the nurse this better be the third and last thing to happen to them. I made her laugh with my stories of the mole showing up and the overuse of Neosporin.

On a positive note: I had two shipments of sundresses from ASOS.com sent to me, and I love them all. I only really want half of them, but that's okay because it's free shipping to and from! Cool thing, too: A few of them, at a size 14, are too big! Yay!

—

Yes, so I love me some ASOS sundresses. So cute and comfy, and I might be a size 10 or 12 in a few of them. This new lifestyle of mine – eating a bit less and doing a bit more – has made me feel better about my surgery and made me feel like I can have the body I keep thinking I'd like to have, even at age 36.

June 21, 2013:

Sidenote:
—Yesterday at Wallymart, sharp pains through rightie for at least five min. Ouch.

June 22, 2013:

I feel very alone. I think I've always felt a little alone in my own family...

Anyhow... I'm hoping we go to Fergus today. I'd like another rhubarb plant and a new something for the big red pot in the kitchen where the dead palm is. If we don't go, I'll go for a bike ride.
I am so very, very mentally exhausted. It's unreal.

June 26, 2013:

I really want to wrap up some grading today (minus Paper 1s??) and then nap and be lazy. Already did kettle bells.

OH, I stepped on the scale and ... we need a new one. That one is so hard to figure out. I might weigh 195 right now or be back up to 200. That thing is not reliable. And I'm okay with only having lost a pound... I can sense that my muscles are coming back, and if I shrink size-wise but not weight-wise, that's okay. Can a woman be around 185 and be a small size 14? It's possible, I suppose. I'd honestly just love to be able to wear a size 14 pair of shorts from Old Navy or the Gap without worrying that I have massive hail damage on my hamstrings. I'd like to be firm and fit and tone everywhere.

Bought the CUTEST vintage dress at Savers yesterday for $3.99 or 2.99 (with 20% off)... it's a faded floral print, but with these leather weird heels I bought, it'll be a funky outfit for Friday's meeting. And I got a pleated, cropped Gap jean jacket in a size Large – no XL anymore? Yay!

Oh, stopped using the cream for the yeast/fungal thing yesterday. It was too muggy and the areola isn't red anymore... It's wrinkly but the same color as the other one. We'll see what 24hrs does of nothing.

June 27, 2013:

I don't know if I really need THAT much more water in my body or what, but I've been getting headaches (towards the front of my forehead) even if I haven't been drinking... super annoying.

June 28, 2013:

Boobie update:
-Saw the red bumps coming back on leftie, so I started the cream again last night. I guess it make take two full weeks to get rid of that crap. And less wearing of sweaty sports bras. I think I'm four months and one week out today. Huh.

Health update:
-I bought a new scale yesterday (purchased odd things at Walmart: scale, temp gauge, smoke detector & a Diet Coke); it's digital! So, I weighed myself this morning since my weigh-in on Wed would've been a big guess (could've been 200 or 195 for all I know) and I'm at 192.8. Now, I highly doubt I've actually lost almost eight pounds since June 5 when I started all this tracking (and when my other scale said 200 on June 5), but whatever!

+It's very windy today, but at least it's cool. The temp downstairs in the house is 75, and part of me wants to do a few reps of kettle bells for my ass, legs, arms and abs and call it good; the other part just wants to be uber lazy today and eat less... I don't know which side will win, but I think I'd like to try to run tomorrow morning especially if it's kind of cool and rainy.

I can't believe July is next week already... oh, hell, I just realized I probably got paid today. And it'll be a big check, too. Yay me!

I think we're (the boyfriend & I) going to have weird times here and there, and that's just how it goes. It's how life goes no matter what. Sometimes you're up or down or just at a consistent spot of happy/contentment. I wish he was at that contentment spot with his life, but I have to be patient that that will happen for him. He has to want it, though, too, so... I can only do so much. I'll start by doing the dishes he left from when I was gone. Then I need coffee and/or kettle bells.

June 29, 2013:

Last night, during my bike ride, I thought about how I wanted to tell him that I'm not a rubber band. Every so often, he pushes me away. It happened when we were living apart and now. And I think he needs to know I won't rebound back each and every time like everything was good during those awkward times. That's where I feel taken for granted. Just give me a teeny bit of affection, man. Good god.

So, after the bike ride, he actually seemed to pay me some attention... he asked me if my bike computer was working okay (such a guy/dad move = don't say you love me, just show me by worrying about things you can fix around me), and we figured out how to get it to go to zero (it was adding up my time; I was at 4+ hours on that thing since he fixed it). Then we looked at the garden. He told me to eat his leftover pizza, and normally I would, but I wanted my cookie dough yogurt real bad.

I had been on my computer in my office before bed...and then headed down to say goodnight, scratched his back in the process of our hug and I said, "Remember when I used to do this?" He said, "Yeah, I call them the good old days." Yeah, the good old days because he had money, and I was broke and struggling. Nice. Oh well, his perspective is his, and I hope one day he fucking sees MINE.

Oh, and on the bike ride too I realized that when I hadn't done super well at my MSCTC interview WAY back in the day, he wasn't like uber supportive about it. I do recall him shrugging it off like oh well. And so I could treat him the same way now, or I could be more mature. (That is a battle, kids.)

So, TODAY, I got up around 8/8:30 and checked the temp (by the way, he had started in bed with me then moved to the den last night and then the couch... weird), and it was breezy and like 60. I thought, "I mentioned in that private FB group that I would try running this morning. And maybe I fucking should." I put on two sports bras (a very basic cotton one and then over the top my hardcore Adidas one) and a cut-off tee (that I had dyed pink & ironed a skull on awhile ago = badass!) and some basic running pants... I even through on my fairly new neon pink Nikes, but laced them semi-loose (heard that's a good idea for running).

It was tough. It wasn't pretty. I was just trying to find my freakin' pace for mile 1 – or almost all of it. I kept running – hee hee – numbers in my head as to where mile 2 started on my route, etc. I was adding up blocks, guessing how long I would take, telling myself that just the fact that I am DOING IT should be enough.

I wanted to stop a lot. Thought about just doing a mile, then just doing 2, but I pushed on. At times, I could feel my legs getting sorer and sorer, but my chest was stable and my lungs felt okay. I think I could've pushed myself into a faster pace, but I also knew that that could be detrimental since it's my first run in a LONG time. I didn't want to overdo it because, well, doing three miles out of the blue is ALREADY overdoing it. Really.

When I got home, I noticed that I was gone for about 45min. Now, I walked over to where my loop starts, and walked slowly back... so I took 5 min off for that and figured I did 3 miles in 40 min. That's not fast, but then I used my computer & www.gmap-pedometer.com to discover that my loop is 3.39 miles. A fairly good 12 min mile... I think my fastest as an adult has been maybe 10, so not too shabby. And to know that at times, I wanted to push myself... that's a good sign, too. AND the chest didn't hurt at all!

Once in the house, I stripped down in the basement and put on new clothing, minus a bra. I felt light-headed all the way until I got horizontal on our bed; this was around 10am. I sucked down some water, had a protein bar and a fiber bar, and after pronouncing my accomplishment on Facebook, I napped for about an hour. It wasn't super hardcore (been noticing that lately – time flies, but I don't think I'm totally zonking out?), but whatever. The boyfriend came to join me around 12:30, and that's when I started to feel like I was good to get up...

He got up soon after, and I think around 1pm or 2pm I made Baked Cauliflower Poppers... from a frozen bag. Too much moisture in them, but they turned out okay. Next time, I'll use fresh.

I still feel like I should accomplish more today, but it looks like we'll watch the Twins and chill in the living room. Part of me is like, "Dude, you RAN today! That's huge after four months & a week of recovery. Just relax!"

June 30, 2013:

He "ditched" me last night to go to "town." I just said okay, and he kissed me goodbye.

Then I made my own plan. I went to the movie The Heat last night (HILARIOUS), and then when I got up this morning, I realized that the pre-50% off sale at Savers (for club card owners) was today. AND that FEED products were going to be at Target. And then I remembered how much I love Clothes Mentor! Yeah. It all came at me at once. So, I took my time finding clothes to get rid of at Savers & put my damn ointment on leftie, etc.

Hit Savers, Target, Clothes Mentor, Platos, then went to see if I had any spray tans left at Sungods… didn't, so I stopped at Moe's for a burrito to GO. Shopping burned a lot of calories – 4+ hours!! – so, I ate the whole thing when I got home.

As I was doing the dishes – I thought we had split up that chore, but it doesn't feel like it lately – I realized he had eaten two of my cobs of corn I got at Econo after the movie AND drank a Diet Dr Pepper (Shasta brand), too! WTF. Plus, he left a mess, really… so, go you Mr. Boyfriend with a fun weekend of drinking and then making a mess for me to clean up. Jeezus christ.

And he's not the only one on my "ugh" list. My sister and my parents and my other sister. Good lord.

And NOW I have to teach that 4-week class tomorrow, and I'm looking forward to it. FORWARD because I'll have a distraction from beating everyone's faces in with 2x4s.

On the way up, I thought, I should tell the boyfriend that we need a plan. He gets a job this summer/fall and then maybe around Christmas/my birthday we elope to Vegas, so that we can start the baby idea up next year… I daydreamed about all this shit, and it went downhill fast when I was exhaustedly driving home AND then when I had to do the dishes. He seems like he's in a better mood, so I'll take one for the team, and I won't blow up at him. Instead, I might hit Cheryl's house for a drink and vent to her.

Ugh.

It's almost comical. My life is practically perfect – I have money and a great job and a boyfriend and a healthy family… yet all these little things are adding up to be an effen monster. If I wasn't so sore, I think I'd go for a de-stressing bike ride. But I am really sore from yesterday and from running around today. Scored some awesome stuff, however!

Chapter 12: July 2013 (Four Months Post-Op).

Originally logged on because my right breast was giving me pains. And in the last few days – since returning to that ointment – my left one has had little shocks of pain go through it too near the fucking nipple. Ugh.

ANYHOW…

I told him I feel alone and not supported. I guess I shouldn't seek out support and, instead, try to find it within, but sometimes a person needs reassurance. Something like, "Hey! OMG, you ran 3+ miles only 4 months after your surgery? Good for you! Glad it didn't hurt the boobies and all that. Yay!" Hmph.

Pre-grocery shopping, he jumped my bones. I saw it coming, and it was good for us. He said he wants to be affection more and if I need more sexy time or just him to rub my belly, I should ask. It's weird how he's gotten more and more lovable as the years have passed.

Then, after we grocery shopped ($118) and liquor shopped, I made myself a drink and tried on all of my ASOS dresses. They all fit = awesome sauce = but some are just EH in my book, so I think I'll keep 3 of the 10 (did I order two groups of 5??).

I had a teeny daydream five seconds ago.

I was wearing the strange white tee I ordered from ASOS recently (has cut out shoulders) & size 12 (or 10?) skinny jeans & those little black strappy sandals (either the Nine West I just bought OR the other old school ones)... and my hair was long & pretty, and I was tone, and I was wearing a small white bra (size 36D?)... it was a cute simple look, and so I think in a minute I'll go for a bike ride even though I already did kettle bells this morning.

I'm thinking of a cookie dough Greek yogurt dinner with a drink or two. Maybe a Weight Watchers frozen chocolate bar, too? Maybe? Yeah.

July 5, 2013:

Well, a month ago (four weeks), I was 200lbs. Now I'm around the 192/191 mark. That's an accomplishment right there. Then add in that I'm back to running 3+ miles and that I can do a plank for a minute... AND I'm using the 20lb kettle bell! Sometimes, you just need a couple of weeks to make a change. I remember thinking I wasn't going to be able to be active daily or track all my food, but I am, and it's nice to have this control over it all.

I haven't stopped using the fungal ointment yet... but yesterday, the boobies went swimming in a lake. It felt great, and it felt cool to "show them off" in a small bikini top. I had no worries that they'd pop out or that someone would think they were too massive (not that it matters what others think, but it's nice to just fit into the crowd sometimes with size)... plus, I was wearing a halter and my neck didn't hurt. Amazing!

Since I ran (3 miles), walked (to the fireworks with my honey and back last night), and swam (treaded water in harsh, windy waves) yesterday all while watching what I ate (let most of my calories go to drinks that I didn't finish), I think today will be a chill day for activity. I was up until midnight, and just woke up around noon to feed Sushi. I am not super hungry yet (ate vitamins & Biotin), so I haven't even had breakfast or lunch.

I should've done a lot of things with this new health plan and with my chest. I should've measured everything and done progress pictures – especially with my breasts – at specific dates/markers of time (2 months, three months, etc.) because they are all over the place. Oh well! I think at some point, when I measured my chest (40″ around the biggest part; 34-36″ around the bottom), I measured my hips and they were 45″… I do believe at one point before the surgery, I was 45″ – 35″ – 45″ = Hourglass! Huh.

July 10, 2013:

Alrighty then… any other things to catch up this little blog with? Oh, he has been giving me ideas for the textbook (focus on students more, etc.), and my chest has still been getting coated with that ointment for the fungal stuff.

I'm still buying stuff from ASOS constantly, but I found some bikini tops that I WANT to wear, and I purchased some gladiator sandals from Free People ($158) that should be super cool for Moondance, etc.

I think I'm shrinking even if the scale on Thursday or Friday morning isn't 2lbs less than last week. I tried on almost all of my jeans, and many of them fit better AND my ass looked better in them. Perky! Yay!

July 11, 2013:

So, when I weighed myself this morning, I wanted to be under 190. But I wasn't. Last night, I weighed like 193 and this morning was 192 until I pooped and took off my compression bra; then I was 191.4… a .2 loss, but probably not a loss because I haven't weighed myself with that little bit of clothing on. Whatever. I'll get to the 180s and then to the 170s. Slowly but surely. It's nice to feel in control of my food and activity and know what my body needs. I should've taken measurements of my arms and thighs (just like I should've done with my chest), but that's okay.

I tried on almost every single pair of jeans in my closet last night; they almost all fit and better than usual. It was nice. Only 8ish pounds down and everything's fitting better on top and bottom.

Tomorrow, I should weigh myself again since I weighed myself last Friday... or maybe I did do it on Thursday? Today, I was a bit below 1200 cal... no exercise because I felt like I overdid it yesterday with that 60min bike ride. My muscles were SO SORE riding. And my crotch, too.

So, I'll wake up... do kettle bells and maybe run up and down the stairs a bit; doing that burns like 900/hour or 158ish calories in 10min! Then shower and teach. I have a buffalo cauliflower bite recipe I want to try for lunch, so I'll hit up Econo after class & dink around the house before I have drinks at 3pm.

July 11, 2013 (Part 2):

Me to my gals via Facebook:
Speaking of boobs, I'll be hitting my 5 MONTH MARK tomorrow. Yay!!! Time flies when you're massaging your chest & hollering at leftie to quit being an asshole.

ANYWAY, I think I should celebrate with others who have boobs. Anyone up for a drink tomorrow evening? I realize people may be heading out of town, but I thought I'd throw out an invite anyhow.

July 14, 2013:

Dear Body,
I'm trying to change you.

I don't want to be scary-skinny, but I want my muscles to come out of their hiding places. I don't want to suck down gallons of water because I'm "supposed to," but rather I want to completely ditch drinking pop daily (I'm almost down to drinking it like every other day IF that). I don't want to give up sweets or feel like I "have to" workout everyday, but instead I want to find balance; desserts aren't necessary everyday, & I shouldn't go weeks without being active!

I'd like to eventually tone myself down to a size 12; that might mean weighing 170 or less (or more? based on muscle mass), but either way, I have a few months of serious focus to go. I'll maintain after with activity & eating low-cal count days (leaning still towards protein & veggies).

Speaking of muscles, I can feel my ass ones trying to pop through. My arms are feeling tough, and my quads/hammies burned during/after today's bike ride.

The muscle(s) above my right breast were sore yesterday; I thought it was a stitch almost. Lately, I have felt little zips of pain go through the bottom of leftie (and sometimes rightie, but it's less intense).

July 16, 2013:

*Sidenote: Stopped putting ointment on my boobies last night. I'm sick of doing it, and it's been a long time. If the damn rash comes back, oh well. I'll go in to see her again.

July 16, 2013 (Part 2):

I jumped on the scale for shits and giggles, post-eating two teeny burgers the boyfriend made yesterday, and it was a little over 190... that probably means that I'm under 190 in the mornings when I've been weighing myself. If I'm a 180-something person by Thursday, that'd be awesome sauce. Then I'd have to watch – well, even if I wasn't 180something – my eating and activity this weekend at Moondance. I think the food will be the biggest issue. To not overdo it and use most of my calories for drinks (and maybe drinking water too in there to hydrate). I hope we do some sort of activity in the mornings like bike on those floating bikes or swim or walk around town. That'll help. Plus, walking and dancing at Moondance should shed some extra calories, too.

If I can stick to drinks and protein and lots of movement, all will be well.

I felt really small – first time in a long time, let me tell ya – trying on my three orders from ASOS today. A small size 10 dress (the numbers dress for Math Olympics next May – yes, that's a ways off, but I assume I'll be this size OR, hopefully, smaller anyhow) fit and showed off my smaller tummy and pumped up ass. A black dress that I sent back – the back was too low – was also a 10 and adorable on me. I got this awesome lace peplum top (in a size 12?) and some skinny jeans (size 14)... it was a big boost to my body-image-ego. Some of their bra tops or bralets just aren't supportive enough, so I think I'll stop ordering them.

I just weighed myself – I don't really have to until tomorrow morning – and I'm under the 190 mark! Yay! It was like 189.6 or something, but I definitely will weigh less in the morning (I would highly assume). To think that the day of my surgery, I weighed in at 207 (or 209?)... I'm almost at that 20 pounds-lost-mark. Oh sure, two of that is the boobies, but whatever.

Gained about two pounds at Moondance. Oh well. My semi-naked body in the mirror this morning didn't show it... no major worries there.

Focus on me: So, I'm supposed to go to Fargo tomorrow morning for another follow-up appointment, but I'm going to try to move it to the following Tuesday because I have class, & I also have a bad sunburn. I don't want the surgeon to be like, "Don't burn your new boobies, you idiot!"

Then I read in my Allure magazine that those people who have mixed emotions about how their lives are going – they aren't just uber positive – are the healthiest because they have that balanced view of everything.

I took a three hour nap yesterday; that shows you how stressed out I am, I guess. I might need another nap today. He's gone until 7pm, and I may hit sand volleyball again... M & M invited me to drink/grill with them before they play at 7:30, so that might be fun. Get out of the house, etc. I need to workout, too. Kettle bells, maybe, and a bike ride? Don't know. And I may wait until Friday morning to weigh-in, so I can get up tomorrow and run instead. I think it's supposed to be cool out.

IN THE FUTURE, I should blog when things are GOOD between us. Remember how we had a silly conversation about my textbook only weeks ago? Or had that talk on the way back from Jilary's about the categories of people? Remember going grocery-shopping and just enjoying doing that together? These things happened days ago & not eons... we'll probably get back to all that.

I like my NYC boyfriend, my at-a-Twins-game boyfriend, my laughing-on-the-couch about something stupid boyfriend. Where the fuck did he go?

We're going to be in trouble if this not-talking thing lasts longer than a week or two, but I'm optimistic that things will return to "our normal." In the meanwhile, I need to rest before school starts up full-throttle in about a month.

July 31, 2013:

Doing an August challenge with the I Can Do This! Group. Should be interesting. I hope I'm 185 by next Wed when we start the challenge because then I might be in the 170s by the end of August.

Woot fucking woot.

Got SO many cool items yesterday.

Bras, for one. I'm a 36D now in Lilyette bras (Olga cups are not quite big enough?); I don't remember the last time I was a single letter! Maybe for 5 months in the 90s?

Cute little jackets & cardigans for school... jewelry from F21... 13 random items from Clothes Mentor (their clearance was $2!)... I spent a lot, but it was a great alone day for me. I had my last follow-up appt, too, and she said to tell the boyfriend "Hi," that he did a great job of taking care of me, that I could wear underwire... and the nurse Erica noticed my weight loss (so she said AFTER I mentioned it). We took after pictures, even. I need to do that tomorrow. August 1st will be five months out. Wow.

Sideboob #5: Maid of the Mono-Boob.

-I could call the book <u>Maid of the Mono-Boob</u>... because of what sports bras do to my chesticles?

-Sometimes, I ask myself: "Did I even look at my boobs today?" Isn't that a weird concern?

-How to start book? "I was supposed to like them. My breasts. But it never really happened. I wanted to velcroe them on & off in high school; I knew they had power over guys, yet I still get jealous when I see a small chested lady in a deep V-tee.

Or...?

-I guess. Must be the next step as they heal. The muscles underneath wake up & join forces with the nerves? (This might've been sent in a text to someone during Week 2.)

-They've gone from itchy to sore. Now, when they hurt, it's like, "Shh, don't move. Don't wake them up." (Week 2)

Chapter 13: August 2013 (Five Months Post-Op).

August 1, 2013:

I took my 5 Month Post-Op pic today. Yep, five months ago today kids, I got chopped up. Huh. They've "dropped" a little bit and yet they are so light that a teeny droop is taken care of with a medium-support sports bra. SO NICE. Also, after taking the pic, I compared it to the others and maybe my weight loss has caused them to shrink a wee bit too. The pics aren't perfectly comparable, but they are less wide anyway. I have a red bra on from Walmart today. It's wireless, and a size 38D. It's large in the cup, but comfy. And red! I tried on my other 38Ds from that Herberger's clearance rack and they are large in the cup, too. The three bras from Kohl's (36Ds) fit okay but the one I didn't try on – a red one – is not a minimizer and doesn't fit perfectly. I'm thinking about hitting that store again this Saturday because I might go to the Pre-Pride Drag show with my sis Saturday night.

My belly is still "out there." I remember not liking that my breasts were small and how that accentuated my gut, but it's shrinking and my chest has shrunk, so yeah. As things shrink, maybe my confidence will expand greatly!

August 1, 2013 (Part 2):

This red bra was bugging me today; I may stick with sports bras for the summer. They irritate me less, and I've been in them for 5 months. Leftie still stings me. Yay?

*Ate about 200-300 over my typical 1200 cal today (got McD's happy meal tonight for the first time in a long time), and I still feel okay.

Tomorrow, I'd like to attempt a Jillian DVD (via YouTube) & then a nice leisurely bike ride.

Life was alright, and then it suddenly got better. He's back at the bar, and that's part of it, and then I keep losing this weight, which is another part of it. So nice that life can turn a corner and feel GOOD. LIFE IS GOOD, kids. Yay.

-A Boobie-Related Thing for my book: It occurred to me the other day that anyone I run into who has had the surgery isn't forthcoming with info, really. Which seems strange to me. Hil's sis was more of a warning sign: "Don't forget the Vitamin E," and a kind of a bragger: "I don't have any scars!"

Then a girl in this health-based private group was like, "I had one, and now I have no boobs at all." At one point, she tried to make me feel shitty for having Ds "left" because hers had done the "mommy thing" and shrunk/drooped... T's aunt was very curious as to what I knew & didn't just throw advice at me. I hope that anyone who asks me about it later, because they are considering it, gets a fresh opinion from me that is uplifting. Yeah. Some women have really made me feel like I am not special to have had it done. I think I have more to say about this, but I'll move on...

I weighed in this morning (switching to Wed weigh-ins for a challenge in that FB group) at 184. Yeah, it was nice to see. I guess sticking to 1200-1500 is better than starving my body under 1200. I bought the UP by Jawbone bracelet, and it should be coming on Friday! That might help me even more, and I figured if it increases my motivation, the $85 price tag will be well worth it.

I missed my pill by 7 hours the other day, so this morning I was a bit freaked. He's been up for more sexy time lately, and we had jumped each other the night before I missed it. The web sites all state that "missing a pill" though means 24+ hours. I suppose it's pretty miraculous if the body can suddenly ovulate in 4 hours or something. So, I put my phone alarm for that back ON. I thought, selfishly to myself when I realized I had missed it, "Man, that would be my luck; to lose weight and then get preggers right in the middle of it all." I KNOW there is more to that whole thing than weight, but that's what I thought. Huh.

Speaking of weight, I probably should calm down on the clothing-buying for awhile. And I don't need more (unless I want to find specific pieces to trade out with crap in my closet)... found four pairs of size 16s at Target for $8 today (then had a Buy1Get1 coupon so they were $6 a piece!). They may end up being the last 16s I need... possibly. Maybe I'll wear what I have until I end up so small I need my "skinny jeans" box? Might as well?!

I should look back in my other blog to see when I was at 184 before and then look at my Facebook pictures for what I was wearing then. I think this time around I am larger because I've been working out. I might need to get to 170 before I fit into the skinny jean box stuff? Or less? Dunno. I do know that I would like to be in the 170s before school, and I wouldn't mind hitting 150 before Christmas.

Anything is possible. ANYTHING.

August 11, 2013:

Life continues on into the awesome sauce category.

He went fishing Friday afternoon through this evening... and I was uber busy, too:

—TEDx was in Fargo Friday, so Cheryl & I were driven up by our bosses' boss (and a student tagged along in the back)... it was fun times. I learned SO much, and it was fun to hang out with my peeps.

Conversation at TEDx:
Me: "Have you lost weight?"
Her: "Yes, like ten pounds. Thanks for noticing."
*She did not return the observation, and I've lost more. Huh.

+ I tried on almost ALL of my jeans this afternoon (took some pics too of outfits) and those black size 14(?) jeggings from The Gap fit. They have been uber tight for awhile now. Crazy stuff! I feel like I really REALLY should consider not buying bottoms for a long while now because I'll be an in-between size. I filled a massively large bag already with jeans I'm not crazy about anymore.

August 13, 2013:

Now cut to me & my stuff. I weigh-in tomorrow for the I Can Do It! accountability challenge... I think I snuck a peek at my weight yesterday morning and saw 183 point something, but who knows what damage (or non-damage) I can do in a day... I think I ate well today, but yeah... I wish I wouldn't freak out about stepping on that scale (and it changes within the five min I stand on it... the 184 from last week was less and more by .2 every min or so... weird damn thing); I also wish I wouldn't think, "Oh, yeah, these ladies who come back to the Facebook group and have GAINED weight – that'll never be me." But it could be. And yet I have the capability to do something about it, so I should just remember that! Errrg.

So, I hope I'm down a pound at least. I think I will be, and yes I'll take 182 too. IF I am down below 184.5 (which is what I averaged from last week because I think the scale was at 184.2 when I first stood on it and then it jumped to 185 later – again, weird ass device!!), then that whole shipment of stuff from Alloy could be up for keeps. That's a good deal, right? I almost feel like I should check my weight tonight to see where I could end up, but that's a little obsessive, isn't it?

When I looked down at my legs tonight, while I was walking, I noticed that my knees appear thinner to me and more muscular. That makes me feel good. I have to focus in on the non-scale victories like that because the number on the scale might not always move down.

Tomorrow, weigh-in... hit campus with a water jug after sending back almost all of that Urban Outfitters shipment... do some work and start to design ways to stay in shape this school year. I know it's MOSTLY about eating, but I'd love to have a walking route on campus AND take more swimming classes!

August 18, 2013:

1. Things are good within me. I feel almost prepped for school. I feel tone. I feel confident. I gained more pairs of jeans last night because I found a box of in-betweens (some 14s and some small 16s) and ALL of them "fit," yet because they only looked "eh," I'm giving some away. Yay, right? I'm hoping to get some cash for them via the place in town that buys clothes OR via Clothes Mentor in Fargo. I might head up Tuesday to hit the latter and Savers and spray tan and drop of Robbie's present. Word.

2. Things are good with him. We hit up FF yesterday to shop for lawn furniture and look at fencing materials and talk "deck" ideas, too. We ate at Don Pablo's (heard some drama there between two customers?) before Fleet Farm (water bottles for Yard Party $2), Home Depot (a bust), Dunham's ($160 for an HRM and an indoor bike), and then back to Fleet for the lawn chairs we saw the first time around ($170). It was a good day... when we got home, we helped ma&pa with a desk for my cousin Jake.

August 18, 2013 (Part 2):

Boobs.
"I haven't looked at my boobs yet today."
I've never had that thought until after this surgery. Yep.

And speaking of boobs, since I feel like posting seventeen times today, I've noticed that any celebration I want to have about those is similar to wanting to celebrate my continued weight-loss. Actually, celebrating the chest might be more welcomed by people... but anyhow, I wanted to post about having gained more jeans last night when trying on the ones in that box from the basement, but I held back & didn't. I could've posted this morning about how these olive green size 16 (Gap?) shorts were uncomfortable on me last summer and/or the summer before that and yet today, they feel fine & just a tad bit big.

And sure part of me worries that I'll "brag" only to watch the weight inch back onto me. But I feel like with everyday that I learn to eat 1200 cal + exercise vs. 1800 cal + not exercise in some capacity, I'm adding more time to the experience of all this. The longer I'm doing this for myself, the longer it'll take to forget it. Fad diets, where you go on it for 6 days and feel like shit and then look great for 1 day, don't give you that experience factor. Like the experience of babysitting... or something like that. If you do that for awhile, you know what it's like. You gain the knowledge it takes to return to it and do it again and again. If you babysit just once, and then never again, it's hard to get back to it.

I don't know if that's a good comparison, but whatever.

I was just thinking today – that WHO KNEW this year would be a great year for me? I didn't at the beginning of the year. I thought, "Well, I won't run the Half with my sis because my chest is huge, and I'm huge," and then my surgery came and went and I thought, "Okay, I love my chest, but my gut is huge now; what I can do this summer? I bet I'll just continue on this path and go back to school in the same rut." BUT NO. And so that's awesome. Yeah. Go ME.

Who KNEW that 36 would be absolutely fucking fabulous?

Remember that magazine article about how many actresses looked great at 36... well, there ya go. And I feel like even though I'm aging, I never want my 20-something body or mind or life. I'm only going up from here.

I'm proud of me. I wanted a smaller chest to help with my back and exercising. So I took care of that. Then I wanted that to be the catalyst into a better body overall, and I am taking care of that too. It's awesome. I finally did things for my body that I should've been doing all along when I was taking care of my mind and getting an education.

And maybe it was meant to happen NOW because MFP didn't exist AND that has made everything uber easy... AND it was meant to happen now because I'm more appreciative of this tone body.

August 19, 2013:

Goodbye Clothes & I Won't Cry.

Tomorrow, I'm hitting Fargo to paint the town a light shade of green... a light shade because I'll be thrifting and not spending tons and tons. Well, it could happen at Clothes Mentor because I'm bringing A LOT of clothing to them for trade. Like 18 pairs of jeans. And many pairs of heels.

AND I'm bringing things to Savers, too. But I think I'll hit CM first because they might not want all my stuff. Then I can try to find thrifty up-scale things first before going to Savers. They are having – Savers that is – a 50% sale on some summer stuff for the Savers Club card members. Yay, right?

I'm excited to PURGE in a good way. Goodbye 18 dresses to Savers. It'll be nice to have COOL things in my closet that FIT me. And when I get home, my honey will be here and my ASOS packages, too! Weee!!!

August 26, 2013:

So, we had that nice night of bonding Friday (or at least it felt nice) and then this weekend we didn't see each other a lot. Saturday, I hit up Fergus to shop and then hit the lake to see Emmett & crew... ended up at the sandbar swimming, and when I got home around 7, he was still here. Turns out he didn't work until 9, but he didn't want to go with me to Fergus anyhow. I think he just sat around all day. It was a hot one, so I probably would've done that too.

As he's getting ready to go that night, he says he's going to stay up there until Monday morning since he has to work at 5 on Sunday. I ask where he's staying, and he says Roger's place. I make a face because we know that he has a crummy basement apt. I was skeptical – like are you staying with a chick and are lying to me? – but most of me (99%) trusts him, so yeah.

ANYHOW, I got up around 7 to bike. When I returned, he had gone upstairs to sleep. I showered downstairs and headed to campus around 9:30. I didn't put out the garbage; I hope he did get up to do that. Whatevs.

Isn't it a bit strange that I get more riled up when I don't see him – yet we have left things relatively fun & good, etc.? Weird, right? Totally. I get myself worked up all the time. ALL THE TIME.

Sidenote on Boobs: In the shower this morning, rightie had like a hard lump in her. And both felt very solid-ish. The humidity? The workout? Don't know...

August 26, 2013 (Part 2):

Let's leave the bloggie with some positivity today, shall we?

I'm wearing these size 16 red Gap shorts from last summer... and they are a bit big in the waist & when I sit down, I don't feel like my thighs are all over the damn place. Plus, worn with my "i before e except after c" black tee, I look very CAMPUS-y. Yay!

So, remember how I noticed that pre-green pill week, I couldn't blog about him and I because that's when I was more emotional (fucking hormones!)? Yeah, I think we are just going to have good times paired with quiet times, and that's how the life we have will pan out... yesterday, he started off a tad bit goofy when I got home (was on campus from about 9:30 until 4:30); he asked if I had class; I said no; he asked if I had class tomorrow (today); I said no. And then he said something like, "Well, I tried."

I got a weird feeling yesterday or today about how he could be just "taking me for a ride" with all this money stuff. Like, he gets to take it easy... he could not pay me back and yet get his truck fixed, and he could be saving up a lot of money hoping to move back to Fargo and impregnate some whore from the bar who he screws when he goes up there. It's possible, I suppose, but highly unlikely. It just shows ya how getting screwed over by other guys fucks up your own head. Based on the fact that we've been together for as long as we have, I don't think that's even a 1% possibility... but hell, I thought my ex was a stand-up guy. He probably did fuck Andrea that night he went on date with her; he said he just showed her his dick, but I bet they screwed. Asshole. At least I never had sex with him.

I am demented.

But I think he loves me and shows me via actions.
And I think we're going to be okay.

When I got home from campus yesterday, he was gone. I went upstairs to put on comfy clothes and close my eyes for a bit. When I came down, he was watching Sports Center, and I think I said, "Hi," and that was about it. I can't recall if we talked much beyond that, and around dinner time, he announced, "I'm going to be gone for a few hours," I said where are you going, and he just said, "Out." Okay?

I just, ONCE AGAIN, can NOT only focus in on him. He gets in these funks every so often. It's like he's having a good time, and then it dawns on him that, "No, must not enjoy myself; life sucks." Oh, I do remember that at some point yesterday – after he gave me the remote and I watched RHOC & Chelsea Lately – that I went up to the bedroom to tell him about the insurance outcome. Before I told him, I laid on him on the bed and he smiled over my goofyness.

Ugh.

Well, let's focus on ME. I'm the one who matters most. And my 8am class went well. I may have given 'em too much info about myself, but oh well. I think one has to lighten up 8am classes as much as possible. I don't forsee any psychos in there either.

Before I "leave" and before I forget = here's a note from yesterday:

Twenty Pound Gift To Me.

Okay, I know that I buy myself stuff a lot, but I think a specific "new item" would be cool as a gift for this loss. And it's ten percent gone... From where I was in June (at 200lbs). So, tomorrow morning I could be down another 2lbs and be at 180. I wanted, semi-badly, to be in the 170s before school started, but I'll take anything less than 182.

Everything I own fits better. Those size 18 shorts from last summer are massive (what if my shorts from this summer are too big next summer?); the red Gap ones are a tad big. It's getting easier & easier to dress myself. Shopping is more fun, too. I mean, it was typically fun before but now it's a blast. And I don't have to grab 16s all the time. Just imagine when I grab for 12s some day...? Weird.

Anyhow, maybe I should consider Fran's necklace, the iPhone case, the Buddha beads, and the Newport heels from eBay as my gift. Or I could order some shit from ASOS? The last order = just kept a bag, right? Huh.

Chapter 14: September 2013 (Six Months Post-Op).

September 5, 2013:

Sleepy Goals.
I hit my 10% goal yesterday; June 5 saw 200lbs. and today saw 179!
I am also about to publish my anti-textbook, too.

The only negative: I'm tired & sore. Can a person experience chronic fatigue from too much exercise?

I have Sept 5 pics to take! Then a morning nap! Then strength training!

September 6, 2013:

I'm on Amazon.com!

Yep. I'm a published author of my own fucking book.

It appears that I don't have a lot of family that give a shit about that or my weight loss, so whatevs. I am so excited for me right now.

I have a cushy job, I have a boyfriend who mostly likes me, I have great health & the body I didn't think I'd really have at 36... I am intelligent, and fun, and blasphemous.

We got our iMacs in on campus today as I was packing up. SWEEETTT, right? Yay! Tomorrow and this weekend are going to be pretty freaking cool. I hope.

September 9, 2013:

"Fat Me."

Everybody likes "Fat Me." This I said to my sister on our way out of BWW yesterday before hitting up the cousins' baby shower. She didn't really argue with me.

I'm guilty of not necessarily wishing people well on their weight loss journeys.

Dana, the newbie in our dept, said that I didn't really put my status out there for reassurance, but more for a "Hey, I hit a goal" reason. She's right. Why can't my family be happy for anything I do?

Ugh. What a headache I get from this shit.

Luckily, it doesn't affect my progress. I still want to prove everyone wrong in the publishing realm and in the fitness realm. If I do that triathlon next August, I might only tell my boyfriend. No one else will care. Hell, they barely cared when I did the Half Marathon.

This could be karma coming back to bite me, and I'm aware of that. Yeah.

September 12, 2013:

Well, I've copied and pasted my journal entries. I started to revise them, too, and create Chapters, etc. I may have deleted too many things because after talking to Dana yesterday, I do agree with her idea that anything remotely related to my surgery and its after-effects should be kept in this book.

I have to write about my mom's body issues, and while I don't think she'll read this book (she's not much of a reader), her issues were passed down to me like her big chesticle genes. By writing about them, I'm not trying to bash what she has said to me or what has happened to her to give her those body issues (perhaps Gma didn't stop the cycle; it is a cycle that parents have to break – what their parents' issues were & maybe by doing this we create new issues... I don't know), but this is my truth.

A fact for me is that I have never been happy in my own skin.

It was told to me early on that I would not be my sister Robin. She was and is lanky. She, as far as I know, doesn't have to worry about what she eats, really. I was never told I was beautiful or athletic. I knew I did the latter – I was highly involved in sports, but I never heard from my family that I was amazing. I had to tell myself those things. When I beat girls in tennis, I had an awesome coach and awesome teammates pump me up, but that was about it.

Again, this isn't a pity party. This is just what I recall happening.

Then in my freshman year of college, I lost weight instead of gained. I was depressed over a break-up. I knew the cause, but my mom was so worried that she mentioned taking me to a doctor. I thought, "Wow, woman. I know I'm not eating, and I know why. Are you concerned for me or for what it will look like to others?"

Later, I'd date a new guy, and he would be my boyfriend all through college. He loved biking, and I was not opposed to that kind of activity. I would tag along with him and his buddies on hour-long bike rides through and around the Fargo/Moorhead area.

Eventually, the "honeymoon" would fizzle, and he'd start commenting on how I'd eat fried food and the hail damage on my hamstrings and how if I listened to him – and he became "my coach" – he'd help me lose weight and tone up. So, I wasn't good enough. I was smart and pretty, but he wanted twenty less pounds of me. At the end of it all, he left me for a former high school girlfriend who told him how she worked out for two hours a day; they eloped, and I hope she doesn't have an eating disorder.

Once he dumped me, near Downer, MN no less, I took a few weeks to not eat and wallow in my sadness. A month later, I was in Battle Lake, MN prepping for my first teaching job ever at their high school. I had an inexpensive apartment in an old house near the lake, my appetite came back suddenly, and I dove into becoming a good teacher.

My weight issues would pop up from time to time there, and when I was let go after my second year there, graduate school became my future. In grad school, I grew my brain and my waistline. My current boyfriend started dating me in 2002 when I was around the 200lb mark. My hair was permed, I had better fashion sense (well, minus the perm decision perhaps), and yet my chest was continually getting in my way. The night we first kissed, he commented on my hair at least 3 times, so I assumed he wasn't much of a "boobs" or "ass" guy.

September 12, 2013 (Part 2):

I needed the surgery, so I would love me for me. I couldn't "keep them," so that others would be okay with me and my body. I don't know if that makes sense, but I've always rebelled against doing things just so that other people would feel okay dealing with me. I have felt this way about my teaching career, my relationship ("Just start hinting that you want a ring." But what if I really don't want to be married and I'm not just saying that to sound "cool"?), my indecision on having kids (I'm supposed to want children; why isn't my biological clock going off?)...

Perhaps this is a lower form of what "famous" people go through. They make it big, and in the eyes of the people around them, they've "changed." They've "gone Hollywood," or something. I'm not a reborn Christian, or someone who is suddenly famous, I'm just someone who is evolving and refuses to make decisions that aren't in my best interest.

Through losing this weight and a chunk of the chest, I feel more able to see what I want in the world, and what I can do to help others. We all want to feel acceptance, but we have to accept ourselves first. And whether someone sees my need to be smaller as a flaw or not (oh, well, she can't love herself unless she's a size ___!), is not what I have to worry about.

September 12, 2013 (Part 3):

I can already hear my sister Robin bitching me out for writing what I've written in this book. "Sybil, why did you have to write like that about mom?" But she doesn't get it. I'm fairly certain she's received positive feedback about her body for her whole life. If not ALL positive, than at the very least, a very large percentage.

Her and my brother Jed don't understand the viewpoint I have on our mother. They don't see what I see or feel.

September 12, 2013 (Part 4):

I tried on the bras in my drawer tonight for the hell of it & didn't notice that leftie was drooping more than rightie... And he's a bit bigger around the bottom... I see this in the bathroom & wonder, semi-panicked (like 5%), what the hell is wrong with him. I hope he's better tomorrow.

I poke around both of them. I do this a lot. I feel small lumps and rock-like creatures. I tell myself it could be cancer. Then I pluck little hairs from the incision areas; they say that if hairs are growing there, things are healing well. Yet we all know "they" say a lot of shit. Don't "they"?

In bed just now, reading & decompressing, I felt a long-term ache in rightie. It just went away, and I grabbed my phone to record it. Of course.

These boobs have a mind of their own. Ya know, should I have been using proper terms for my chest this whole time? I mean, they are just words (says the English teacher)... And it's my story. Oh snap!

September 13, 2013:

False alarm on the left titty. I just needed to rest. Like all swelling – I've noticed that I drop 2 or more pounds by sleeping – it disappears at night.

Speaking of sleeping, I can't recall if I've written about this yet, but as I was zonking out – and I have been very tired lately; so much so that falling asleep at night is easy & during most of the day (whether I workout hardcore or not in the mornings), I could nap at a moment's notice – I thought of lying on my right side to counter the puffiness of leftie. It's like that whole M&M theory; when I eat them, I need to put equal amounts on each side of my mouth... as if getting cavities should be a balanced endeavour? Anyhow, I have felt that way about my chest as well. I just slept on leftie for half the night; time to flop on over and smoosh rightie. I have noticed the strangest things about my body and mind throughout this whole recovery.

Goodness.

Oh, and as I said in my last entry, I tried on the bras in my drawer (mainly to see if I could fit into any of my old ones at all & to donate others – compression bras, larger sports bras from earlier on, etc.). I did kind of fit into a 34DDD bra, but it was comical how high up the cup went... I mean, I have nothing to fill the damn things out with anymore. This made me smile, a good thing before bedtime.

I put a few 34G bras in a donation bag. I had kept them around because they were so gorgeous (and expensive), but what's the point? IF I ever become that large again, I'll buy new ones. And that IF is such a small possibility. I also chucked a 38C bra in the bag; I have shrunk enough around myself that the band was too large; I might have small boobies, but they still need support damn it. Duh.

*Well, I wanted to focus on this book (since I just published my anti-textbook) for awhile, but I'm thinking I should try to throw together my anti-textbook of creative writing WHILE I add more and more entries to this bugger. As always, I have too many ideas in my head.

September 17, 2013:

Well, I royally flipped out on my 3pm class yesterday. I dropped the f-bomb for the first time ever. I know, I know, not very "lady-like," right? Oh well.

Then I got home. And flipped out on the boyfriend. It was an accumulation of so many things... in the last few weeks, he's done very little communicating or caring for himself and me. So, a stream-of-consciousness came out of my mouth.

"You drank my vodka, so are you an alcoholic now?"
"I told Alisa the other weekend that if you suddenly told me you had another girl in Fargo and were going to move back there, I would be relieved."

After my verbal word dump, I left to attempt to get groceries.

I ended up in the Walmart parking lot. Just sitting there. I didn't cry. Instead, I could feel my blood "boil" as they say. I text KJ and Cheryl. They tell me to meet them for a drink. I do. I vent.

Cheryl and I ordered food to-go and ate/talked at her place. Once her daughter Lizzie got home, I headed to my home. Her last piece of advice was to tell him to marry me or leave me. I said that I appreciated her outlook, but that that was a wide range of possibilities. I mean, I know I go "from A to Z" quickly, but you can't tell me that there isn't some grey area in all this... in ALL of life.

In fact, the longer I am here on this crazy earth living, I have noticed that things have so much grey area to them it's hard to stand in the middle and see white on one side and black on the other. Just look at my recovery, did I completely remain a "T-Rex" everyday? No. Was I lifting chubby kids all day either? No. Grey area. Did I put Vitamin E oil on everyday? No. Did I neglect the skin where my incisions are? No.

And, sure, I like grey area because it's a happy place to be. Dark grey can turn to black in a heartbeat or white can become silver over time. How did this entry suddenly become about monochromatic things? Weird.

Anyhow, once home, I told myself that I just had to talk this out with him. I had mentioned to the girls that I love to employ the silent treatment, but they agreed with me that this was the time to pounce and get shit out. I sat on the long couch, asked him to turn down the TV, and I talked to him some more about everything. He finally tells me that he doesn't see three things changing in his life; he doesn't see himself with a job he loves, with a family, and he's certain he will always live "here." Now, I could take offense to the last one because I love the house I found for us, but he also might have meant Wahpeton? I told him that I was concerned about the first one because we could have seventeen kids and three homes, but I don't want to come home to a grumpy ass.

When he said "family," I did feel my heart skip a beat. I'm still unsure if that means I don't want kids or the prospect just simply frightens me. I told him too much, but I did tell him how frustrating it was to be "the glue" in the relationship. How I don't want to be the only one who makes sure we kiss/hug goodnight. How I shouldn't have to be the one to initiate sexytime when it's officially been months since my surgery (he was good about waiting for me to be ready post-surgery).

What I fear is that change won't occur without some sort of breakup. And, yet, I love myself more than I love him.

Jeezus Martha and Mary.

Maybe, just maybe, this short fishing trip with his dad will do him some good. Maybe his dad will say, "Ditch her and figure out your life," or he'll focus on how good I am for him, and how I can help him figure out his life. Obviously, I'd love for him to smoke less, drink less, and go on stupid bike rides with me. I'd also like him to get more schooling, so he can become his own contractor or electrician and make his own hours and all that jazz. He has the genius, but not the ambition. Why is it that those things rarely sit in one person at one time?

It ended with me realizing that I was exhausted. I think we talked for over an hour and a half. He mentioned a few times that he figured a break-up was inevitable, and that was strange that he figured I would just give up on him – or perhaps he had given up on himself and us? But I told him I wasn't going to break-up with him once he returned from his fishing trip. I might have said, jokingly, "Well, we could try to figure out if a break-up is necessary before the holiday season because I know how much you love doing stuff with my family." And, "So, how long do we give this? A year." He doesn't like timelines, perhaps, but it's not like financially he can sit around for a few more months. And if he wants a family with me, that whole job thing needs to be in play before we get hitched and start popping out kiddos.

This, and everything else on my plate, is too much for a Tuesday morning. For real!

p.s. I smell like a pool. Water aerobics was helpful. The instructor, at one point, said we should punch the water and work out our frustrations. So, I did.

p.p.s. My stomach is in knots, still, and last night I think I pooped more than I slept. At least, if it comes down to a break-up, my appetite will die, and I'll lose even more weight. That's a small consolation prize, however, for how shitty break-ups can be. And this time, if it happens, it'll be harder with all his stuff and lack of place to bring said stuff to.

Well, I did a lot of thinking while he was fishing with his dad. The realization set in that I'll be okay no matter what. At least I'm not a woman who has to have a man.

So, they got home while I was at deep water aerobics class Wednesday night. Once I was home, we grilled up some awesome corn and pork chops. Before they looked at Jan's small pickup (brake issues), we watched a documentary on Jim Thorpe. Jan commented on how he was, apparently, not a good father. And I noted to myself that this Jim guy was not a great hubby either, but hey, when you are super in one category of life, it's tough to be super in all categories. I don't think that was a genius sentence at all.

Nope.

Anyhow, things feel okay between us. I've been too tired to bring up much since my Monday blow-up. We cuddled yesterday afternoon, pre-meeting for me & pre-leaving for work for him, and giggled about lube and how I suck at foreplay-talk. I told him about this weird stuff I got at a sex toy party called Nipple Nibbler. I think it's meant to be used on the breasts and elsewhere, and I told him how it tastes good so dudes can lick it off, etc. Before we "parted ways" to get to our destinations, I told him I'd try to find it, so we could play with it this afternoon/evening.

I did find it, and some other crap that can be licked off a person (powdery stuff that went everywhere!), and put it on my nipples as a test run. I did "nip out," but couldn't feel it. I texted him as much while he was at work. I'm partly evil that way.

From sex to babies? Very linear!

I saw a <u>TIME</u> magazine on my officemate's desk this morning. It was on a pile of 'em, and the headline was: "The Childfree Life." I immediately swiped it and put it on my desk. The first paragraph has a woman saying how she felt she just never got hit by the "biological lightning bolt." I concurred in my head. Another chunk of a paragraph that hit me:

"Gerson says that women are living in a 'damned if you do, damned if you don't' social context in a country that she believes emphasizes self-sufficiency equally alongside a deep commitment to motherhood. The mix breeds impossible conflict. Without independence, we're failures. With it, we're selfish" (43).

Lastly, why is it that we ask, "Why don't you have children?" instead of "Why do you have children?" I get the feeling that my boyfriend has succumb to the societal pressure that if we didn't have kids, we'd look like weirdos. Selfish weirdos?! If I remember correctly, his reasons for kids was because of how we'd look to others. That and, "Don't you want a mini-you running around?" Um, sometimes yes, but mostly no.

I don't want to say it, but I think most women would concur that they do the bulk of the work when it comes to raising their children. Sure, there are some awesome dads out there doing as much work if not more with their children, and my boyfriend claims he'd do a lot. But the guy loves to sleep in right now. He likes to do things by himself, without me. As it looks from my viewpoint, it doesn't look like he'd change. AND I refuse to be guilt-tripped into anything... yeah. If the subject comes up again, I guess I'll have to say, "Thanks but no thanks." Down deep, I really don't know if he's all that into the idea either. For him, it might be the thing he feels will fulfill a life spent at the bar. The thought that, "Well, I didn't do anything important – in my eyes – professionally with my life, but I had children and that's something."

I just saw a quote on Facebook:
"Without acts to back it up, words are empty."

September 23, 2013:

I wrote in my iPhone's notepad yesterday that while I don't typically give into peer pressure, I definitely put a lot of self-pressure on my own shoulders. Case in point: Saturday morning, I made a bet with myself to run 3 miles in exchange for doing my squat & ab challenge pieces (180 squats? Etc.). So, I ran. And I'm still sore. I think I might have run 10-minute miles, which is insane to me after having been biking forever and maybe was able to pull out an 11-minute mile at my last 5K.

And beyond the fact that I have the power to lift that self-pressure from my body and mind, I also know that no matter what I have to take care of myself. I cannot allow myself to be pressured into doing something – as serious as parenthood, for example – FOR someone else. And while I love him, we are not married. Then again, even if we WERE, I don't think I would be obligated as his wife to give him a child. Is this the 1950s? No.

At this point, during some overwhelming periods of thinking too heavily about all this, I have come to the realization that I don't care if I look selfish to others in not having children. I'm not selfish. I love children. I just don't think that whole thing is for me, or even US right now. If I become 50 and want little ones around, I'm sure I could become a foster mom.

But – and here's another point – if a person can not see themselves owning dogs or being a foster parent, doesn't that mean you're probably not up for the challenge of being a parent. Yes, those things – dogs and foster children – are not "your own," but they encompass all that parenting is: responsibility and discipline and energy and time and patience.

Maybe I should even be rethinking my, "I want three big dogs" idea. Christ!

September 24, 2013:

Who knew that a breast reduction would lead me to thinking about what my role is as a human on this planet. I mean, I know it's not to reproduce (because I'm not religious enough). Isn't it to simply help those around me? Leave the world a better place than when I came into it? What is the role of a human? What are our duties?

September 26, 2013:

The two pairs of bikini bottoms that were a wee bit tight on me in June are, um, almost too big. How did I find this out? By just tossing them into my pool bag (pre-water aerobics Tuesday morning) and then putting them on in the locker room only to go, "Oh shit." I had to hold up the front a bit before I got into the pool. Thank god I have that class with cute, little old ladies. A wardrobe malfunction would've barely been noticed. Probably.

So, I demonstrate the issue with the bikini bottoms to the boyfriend Tuesday evening. I bet you can figure out where that lead us.

And the same freakin' thing had to happen this morning. I threw stuff into a bag before my bike ride, including the second bikini set I bought this summer (the green pok-a-dotted top was from Old Navy whereas I scored the green pok-a-dotted bottoms, full coverage kind, from ASOS.com). Well, yeah, I get up to Blikre and the damn bottoms are a bit big. It's like, "Um, duh, Sybil. You have lost weight. What did you think was going to happen? You are an idiot. A smaller, tone idiot, but still an idiot."

I guess there are worse things in the world. Like the young girl I saw getting dressed in the locker room who had sort of a furry backside. Not only did I think, "Wow, and my sister thinks she's a hairy woman," but I thought, "She's adorable, and she's got extra hair. Huh. Big fucking deal."

This made me think of when I had a large chest. And weighed 200lbs. I was still a happy camper with my life as it was and is. I still had days, even a few summers ago playing sand volleyball, when I felt small on top and had nights, too, when I'd dress up and feel very pretty. I suppose having long hair helps; I've always been the most vain about the dead hair on my head.

So, no matter my size or weight, I have to remember that what is on the inside really, really truly is what should matter to ME. Sure, it should also matter to everyone else, but society is not kind to us. This is why we have to be kind to ourselves. That's kind of a no-brainer, isn't it?

Oh, meanwhile, the boyfriend is jokingly convinced I'm slimming myself down in the hopes of finding a different boyfriend. Like I have the time or energy for that! But it's a cute worry; he does get jealous once in awhile.

September 30, 2013:

So, the big seven-month marker is tomorrow. I'm in bed, about to zonk out, and I had to note this: I'm still feeling strange shooting pains every so often, usually out of leftie but just now, lying in bed petting Sushi, one came out of the side of rightie (near armpit). And again. And again. I rub it, wanting to say, "You win, now go away."

Chapter 15: October 2013 (Seven Months Post-Op).

It's Pink Twin Tuesday for Homecoming Week. I found four plain white men's V-neck tees in my home office closet, so over the weekend I dyed them pink (found leftover pink fabric dye, too; who has that stuff lying around? For pete's sake!) and then used my stencils and fabric spray paint to create the word GEEK on every single one. The other two female full-time English teachers who are on campus, and the lone sciencer Cheryl, and I are wearing them today with jeans and tennies. We are the Pink Geek Quadruplets!

Woot woot?!

Anne & I are in the two medium tees I had. It's weird to be a medium, let me just say. Someone on that Facebook health group mentioned that they are now in large tees, and I thought, "Yeah, me too!" But then, "Oh wait, no, I'm wearing mediums now, too." It's like my brain's image of my body needs to catch up to the facts. Duh.

THEN we take a picture of our foursome. Well, we had a student do it, and he took a few. I had forgotten that I put my seven-month boobie pictures on my damn iPhone (yep, the one he used to take the pictures), and luckily he didn't see them, but as Cheryl grabbed the phone and swiped THERE were my boobies. We all laughed, but good lord do I need to hide those freakin' pictures better or what? I mean, for real. No one needs to see them. They are teeny to me now – yay yay yay – but I don't need to be slutty about it. If ladies in the future want to check out the before & after, cool, but sheesh.

I'm back from the TYCA-MW conference in Normal, IL. I could've blogged there, but I was honestly too busy. So, I'll try to recap things:

I got as far as Baraboo, WI on Wednesday night. I stopped to shop at Savers off of 694 in the twin cities, and I also shopped at the outlet mall near Baraboo. I think I was still shocked at the sizes I'm fitting into on top and bottom. At the outlet mall, I hit the LOFT and put on a Medium top (wearing it right now) and size 12 pants. Both fit just fine. It amazes me what I've done to my body on my own and with the help of an awesome surgeon.

I felt pretty awesome about myself all weekend, actually. Not too egotistical, just more, "Hey, I'm going to take the stairs up to my room on the fourth floor," and "I'm going to skip drinking one more free glass of wine and hit the pool for 15 minutes," and "I'll get up and bike in the hotel's fitness room for 25min before I get ready for the day." It's amazing what 15-30 minutes of some daily activity can do for a person.

And as far as the chest goes, I did notice that my incisions would get reddish in appearance directly after being in the hot tub. I noticed this in Baraboo after I conducted my own water aerobics in their pool; I also noticed this in Normal in the Marriott pool. I'll admit that I was a bit freaked out because the incisions have been so pink if even visible at times. The redness does go away, but I did make note of it. And oddly, since I wasn't in a hot tub post-surgery until now, I guess I didn't know what to expect. I don't even think I asked the surgeon about hot tubs; I recall asking if I could go swimming (This summer? Only a few months post-op?)...

As I was unpacking last night, Jan asked how many pairs of jeans I purchased. I defended myself with their low prices, but then I said out loud that if I do continue to lose weight, I might not wear the ones I purchased this last week for very long. I think my top will remain a medium, but that's just my guess.

He ended his goofy interrogation with, "Well, I think most guys would be happy that their girlfriends are buying clothing that makes them feel better." I look at it this way: I have to return things to Forever 21 (I bought jeans from them online, and the back pockets are weird) and Charlotte Russe, so that money will come back to me. I also have a TON of items in the basement waiting to be taken to a Clothes Mentor, so that might be a way for me to make money off of all this.

Then again, if I have money and I'm doing just fine paying off my bills, should I feel badly for spending money on myself every so often?

October 14, 2013:

We got some really shitty family news over the weekend, and it's making me grateful for my "boring, little life" right now. Last night, after talking with the boyfriend about the family news – and gaining a new perspective on it all, really – we watched football, and I think I felt myself worry about the family situation while he was consumed with what his new job would entail. Oh, yeah, he landed a job in Fargo as a shop manager for a growing company. I think he's rather pumped about it, and I really think it'll be something he enjoys daily even if there is an hour commute involved.

According to him, in about a month, we'll figure out our budget situation. He wants to pay down all our credit cards, my financial aid, the mortgage, and consider getting himself a good mileage vehicle (and maybe an SUV for me?). I really just want to save money for our future cabin. And maybe that means I should shop a little less. Ugh.

Speaking of shopping, my body keeps shrinking so I had to bring back size 16 jeans to JCP this weekend & get the 14s. I stared at my ass in the fitting room; it's strange to be a 14 again because for the longest time I thought, "It'd be cool one day to be a small 14" and now I am. I almost fit into a pair of 12s at American Eagle at that outlet store in Wisconsin. Okay, I actually could've worn them because they weren't ugly-tight, but yeah. And I did buy one pair of 12s at Old Navy. I don't think I've thrown them on yet, and I hope I don't wait too long to do so because I could shrink enough to make them un-skinny-jeans if that makes sense.

With all the stress the weekend brought, my appetite wasn't there AND my chest was achey. Due to October being Breast Cancer Awareness month, on Facebook I saw that Sunday was "no bra" day. Well, I wore a light-support sports bra all day after my morning bike ride. It's strange STILL to barely wear a bra and not have things all over the place.

I thought to myself last night, even, before zonking out about how I'd look in the bedroom mirror at my large chest and just sigh.

October 18, 2013:

Last night, while prepping for bed, I brushed my teeth and then thought, "I'll lube up the ladies." So, I put Bio Oil on them and under my eyes.

Every so often, I find myself having to reach behind me (like when I'm on the couch & have a glass of water on the coffee table) and thinking, "I hope I'm not stretching out the incisions" or something to that effect. I am pretty "healed up" at this point, but I still worry.

I think there are a few givens for awhile now: they will feel lumpy & I will have slight worry about them.

October 23, 2013:

I had to bring up a trunk-load of undies to Fargo yesterday (a strangely necessary activity post the Get Your Panties in a Bunch volleyball game), so I decided to also bring up a lot of clothing that I no longer wear or fit into (meaning: too big) to Clothes Mentor*. After spending two hours there, I hit up Target and Kohl's and then Savers.

*I brought in two bags & four Rubbermaids which "made" me $230+. I spent $190 of that on sweaters and two coats and a beanie and a few tops...

At Kohl's, I purchased six pretty (and well-structured) bras – mostly by Olga. They were all 36Ds. I think a 34D fit me okay, but it wasn't comfy, and the one 36C I tried on didn't have quite enough room in the cup. They are gorgeous, and I was so happy to just grab a size and put them on and have them fit immediately. No tugging, no hoisting, no adjustments to be made to the actual breast tissue to make it fit... sure, all those bras were $150+ but I got six and not 3!

Bonus = I was able to get mostly colored bras; I needed some mainly for under white shirts, so I got pale pink and even the beige one had pretty lace on it – smaller bras are always prettier no matter the color! When a woman is a size G, there ain't much lace or pattern going on, and when it came to colors, I got to choose from beige, white, and black. I bought a navy one yesterday (wearing it right now – so soft!) and a red one with black lace and, yeah. It's all fabulous. I love my "baby boobies," as I call them.

Backtrack: I was also able to fit into size MEDIUM sweaters at Clothes Mentor/Savers. Crazy, right? I think I'm wearing a black cable-knit MEDIUM right now, in fact. And, as far as bottoms go, I purchased two size 14s (second hand from the Gap) & a pair of size 12 denim trousers (by Michael Kors?). So, even with the gain of a pound this morning (yep, first time since June that the scale hasn't sunk), I'm feeling pretty good about all that I've accomplished even if it means giving away a lot of clothing!

October 28, 2013:

Over the weekend, it occurred to me – even more so – that I am on my own in many respects of my life. I say that, yet one should understand that I don't include my boyfriend in that sweeping generalization. I'm on my own, definitely, when it comes to my body and it's changes. Here's what I mean:

Very few people in my family cared that I reduced my chest. My grandmothers – or at least one of them – did send me well-wishes beforehand, but other than that, the only person to ask consistently how I'm doing has probably been my sister-in-law and then Alisa (the second in command). As I have lost weight, that number is even quieter. Hilary did ask what I was doing to shed the lbs. this weekend, and I gave her the shortest version of the whole ordeal because I feel like I'm bugging her more with that info than any teaching story I have.

That's another thing: I never feel like my stories are worthy. I found myself summing up a situation I had in class with the girls at the hockey game Saturday night even. It's like I've told myself no one cares about my job, so don't bother them with it. Yet, I do use my job to get out of events. I guess it balances out somewhere?

So, not only did that dawn on me this weekend, but it was smacked upside my head again that my mother can not be happy for other people. She's been skeptical of my boyfriend's new job, and when I was hanging with her and my pregos sis Robin Saturday, Robin commented on my weight loss.

"Have you lost weight?"
"Yes, a little."
"On purpose?" I laughed.
My mother proceeds to NOT compliment me in this moment, but instead push against my upper back in a gesture that I read as, "Well, you might be thinner, but your posture is horrible. I shall now be critical of this."

Total Freaking Sidenote: I think it has happened before Sunday's mini-run (I wanted to test out a 1-mile loop around our neighborhood), but I have noticed achey moments in both breasts, particularly under the armpit area. It's like they see a wee bit too much action, and they get lumpy and pissed off. I even wore a pretty strong/tight sports bra yesterday. I still freak out a bit about jolting them around too much, but I do think that's a "good" worry?

Chapter 16: November 2013 (Eight Months Post-Op).

So, yesterday evening, I was trying to tell Cheryl & KJ about the achey-ness I've had in rightie lately. The only problem was that we were belly-up at the bar, and the bartender – newbie – would not take the hint that we were having a semi-private conversation about my chest. Okay, maybe it's my fault for talking about this stuff in public, but he was just standing there listening in on what we were talking about. I should've known better; this is the same guy who talked the whole time Tina & I were in the bar a week ago. Her and I were just wanting to chat with one another, and he was butting in with his own stories. Dude, I didn't come here to talk to YOU.

Anyhow, I tell the girls that this whole month-long Zombie Challenge (that I found on Facebook) has taken a toll on me. My chest is achey, and I am so glad today is a fucking rest day. SO GLAD. JOYFUL, even.

Yesterday, once at home, I also posted a question to a breast-reduction forum I've been poking my head into from time to time. I finally asked if anyone else had crazy fears and worries about the boobies "coming back"?! I know they aren't magically going to fatten up overnight, but I have to mention how this is a worry I have. Gaining weight – after losing almost thirty at this point – or getting pregnant... I don't want to worry so much about those things. And if the latter were to happen in my life, I would want it to be a happy one – or as happy has it can be – without my body image struggles screwing up the whole ordeal.

Like, I have no control over a major event happening in my life – something like a death or car accident, etc. Those kinds of things have the power to change one's thinking and one's motivations and routines. Who is to say that something like that couldn't happen and then throw me into a tailspin of weight gain and then BAM, size Gs again. God, I think I would be so depressed. And it would be two-fold; I'd be depressed from the event and from the weight gain. Ew.

Leave it to me to think about these things before noon on a Friday. I think these fears should only be brought up after a drink with great friends surrounding you because that way someone says, "Oh, jeezus, Sybil. You are tough, and you will be just fine. Live in the moment NOW." And they would be right.

Living in the moment right now means dealing with sunburn. Yes, I live in North Dakota, and it's November. I got the bright idea yesterday to go tanning because I have many minutes left at one of the salons in town, AND I thought it'd be nice to give my body – that has worked so hard – a little warmth & glow. Yeah. I'm crispy. I can not wait for 1:30pm to roll around today. By that time, I will have finished my classes, some grading, and met with an advisee. I need rest. It's my first rest day in 31 days, and my muscles AND SKIN need this rest day to live up to its full potential. Duh.

November 8, 2013:

Recently, on Facebook, there's been a video circulating of this surgery room. The lady about to undergo a double mastectomy is dancing with her surgeons to some song – I think it's Rhianna? Anyhow, it got me thinking of cancer. I know I don't have breast cancer, and I didn't reduce my breasts for that reason, but I'm glad that I went through the same procedures and thought processes for the small amount of time that I did.

At the age of 36, I had a mammogram. At the this age, I also had to have the inner conversation with myself as to what I'd do if the results of that mammogram came back badly. And I'm so vain about my fucking hair that that is what would worry me the most. Chop of the boobies, but don't let me lose my goddamn hair. Sad, right? Totally. But that's where my thoughts go. My thoughts do also go to, "Could I die now and be okay with it?" That is a yes. It's been a yes for awhile, actually. I love my life. I have a legacy in my books and my teaching. I have loved people and have done the things I wanted to do. What more is there? A cabin. Retirement. Five big dogs. More books to publish. More traveling to do. More students to affect.

Yeah.

I am so close to the 160s I can feel it. This morning, I felt really small, so I jumped on the scale and saw 170. Yep. I can't recall the last time I was 160anything.

Then I hit up water aerobics. My one pok-a-dotted top must have shrunk because my boobies wouldn't stay put inside the fabric; I say "must have" shrunk because I know they are not increasing in size*. Towards the end of class, she had us take those boards (kids use them to learn kicking techniques?) and put them under our armpits for arm exercises. I made due, but I could feel the board rubbing against my incision, so I barely got into that exercise and pushed the board into my skin.

*Then again, when I put on my bra this morning (a pretty lacy pale nude one, 36D), I had to adjust the side boob area on leftie. I'll have to just pay attention – but not worry – to these things. Leftie is a bit bigger, and droops a bit lower than rightie. I still have dog ears, too, but with all the oils & lotions I use (which are heavy in Vitamin E), the scars are pinker and pinker everyday.

November 18, 2013:

I'm researching images on Pinterest for both my Creative Writing & World Literature classes. I just came across an e. e. cummings quote that states: "Your head is a living forest full of song birds." I have to smile because I was just thinking this weekend about how I needed to continue blogging.

The blogging web site I starting using in 2002 for two blogs - a private one and a public teaching one – has become "dead" sort of. And when I set out to write this book about my breast reduction surgery and its pre- and post- issues, I used my private blog to journal my thoughts. So, now I've most recently turned to this manuscript to journal what I'm feeling and thinking about everything. I want most of it to connect, obviously, to the surgery and its aftermath, but I'm starting to think I may need another source for non-boobie stuff.

Yeah.

Anyhow, on Friday, it was announced who got into our campus' Leadership Academy this time around (I was not chosen for the first batch two years ago, and yes, I was semi-upset about it), and this time I got in along with some very cool people. These cool people & I hit up one of the pubs in town, and after texting my bf the news (and to, obviously, inform him that I wouldn't be home after work), he surprised me and showed up at said pub. It was a really nice surprise.

I mention this because in the private blog I would often only comment on "us" when things were crappy. I detest that. Even if my best poetry and writing has come out of me when I'm pissed and depressed, I need to really, really focus on the good shit. So, I'm putting it here to remember it. Yeah.

I also want to remember this: I had a conversation in my head while driving to and from Fargo yesterday. In fact, this conversation has been occurring a lot in my melon. I can't seem to drop a few conversations. They all show up as commercials do = they are annoying, and they get stuck in there like a fucking theme song.

The one commercial is the "baby – yes or no – commercial." It contains two ladies who look like me, and they are battling out whether to have one or not and then in the background, there are mumblings from these random society members. You know, old white guys who think women should procreate and hang out in kitchens and just deal with their hubbies going away on weekends to hunt because "that's how it works" or "that's the way it's always been." This commercial sometimes changes into a gender dissection of Ph.D. possibilities. The other commercial is health-weight-body-related, but I'll get to that in a second.

So, Lady Gaga's new album has a song called "G.U.Y." and for me, it's about the girl being "the guy" in the relationship and having control. This lead me to think about – see how this spaghetti works (see studies and literature about how women have spaghetti brains and males have waffles)! – how the X chromosome is found in both males and females, and yet males – with their damn Ys – are considered superior (in a patriarchy such as ours); HOWEVER, they are really the abnormal gender. They have the oddball combo of chromosomes, and yet they get to run things? Think about it. Are they superior, beyond the physical shit?

They don't pop out kids or multi-task or care about people the way most women do. I know I know I know I am generalizing, but for reals. Would we have half the wars if women were in charge? And you can point out, like the commercial in my head would, that women fight other women but really it's a distraction that has been created by men. The red herring. "Let's give them low self-esteem and then they'll worry about how their appearance & compete with their own kind. They'll leave us alone, give us blow jobs, worry about their stupid weight, etc. etc. all because they think the real 'enemy' is other women."

There are no enemies; there are just people who were given control and power who don't have a fucking clue how to use it correctly and appropriately for the good of EVERYONE on the planet.

I might be right on that one. How does this clusterfuck relate to my chest? Well, I did it because I wanted to, for one, but I also can say it wasn't because I feel competition with women who have large chests or small chests – I only feel competition from smart ladies... but that competition usually leads me to wanting to suck their brains of knowledge.

Honestly, when I see a woman with a massive chest, I judge her and think she's sloopy, or that she might not be smart, or she might be using those jugs to get attention, BUT I know women of all sizes who do that crap. And why do I think that? Probably TV and my own dumb judgmental views that have developed. Did I care about others' chests in high school? I don't think so. All I can recall is this one girl who got her boobies early on in like 5th grade, and I felt badly for her. The attention, the early back problems. Ew. Ick. No thanks. I felt pity.

And why do little girls want their boobies to "come in"? To get attention? To fulfill something in them? "Okay, I have boobies; I am a woman now." Is that similar to becoming a mother? "I have to get pregos, so I am a mom and other moms won't be able to judge me." If women are having babies for that reason, holy shit balls.

And now back to the other commercial in my head. I have hit that part of my weight-loss journey where I feel like I have hit a plateau whether I have or not. I was down a few pounds last week, but I am starting to count fucking calories in my head, and I didn't want to do that. At all. Just like I didn't want to be hung up on 36D. "I'm not a C. Oh shit. What if they grow into DDs?" Now it's also – yes, in addition – "Oh, crud, I ate 1350 calories today instead of 1200." As much as I love a good chart (see my Master's Thesis research) or statistic, I can not handle all these numbers in my head.

36. Too old to have kids? (Wait, do I want them?)
1200. Gotta eat that or below to lose weight!
170. Can I comfortably lose more weight or will I be in the 170s for the rest of my life?
12. Will I ever be a size 10? And I never thought I'd be able to buy size 12s to begin with...
34G. Never, never again, please.

It's exhausting. And I know I'm putting a lot more pressure on me than anyone else ever would. Why do we do this to ourselves?

November 19, 2013:

I want to shrink my body & maintain it.
I want to grow my brain & maintain that.
I want to shrink the negativity in my mind.

And I want to give my creativity variety.
Amen.

November 24, 2013:

Achey breasts yesterday shopping & today... Will they always pop in & out with aches? Did they ache before?

I paid no attention to them before. Good god.

Chapter 17: December 2013 (Nine Months Post-Op).

Usually, when I'm about to get my period - leftie (& sometimes rightie) will feel lumpy-er than usual or those lumpy pieces feel very dense at times.

Last week, I kind of doubled up on "workouts" because of the snow we got. I had water aerobics for 50 minutes on Tuesday (Dad's 60th birthday) and then shoveled for about an hour on top of that. I didn't have to, because we have a blower, but I figured the fresh air (this was pre-below zero temps) and the variety of exercise would be good for me. Well, not only did the extra exercise cause my back to ache, but I woke up with my chest hurting Wednesday along with a stomach ache that I can only attribute to the stress from dealing with two helicopter parents – moms, that is – early in the week.

I think I even ended up writing to someone on Facebook about how my stress shows up in my boobies now. That person said something like, "The boobies know!" and I thought, "Yes, they do." So, I called in sick on Wednesday (I still don't think my boyfriend knows I did this because he leaves so much earlier in the mornings now than I do) and took ibuprophen for the first time in a LONG time.

I didn't really learn my lesson, of course, because I doubled-up again on Wednesday afternoon or maybe it was Thursday. Yeah. Only that time, I stopped shoveling after 30 minutes because my left knee cap twisted itself mid-snow toss.

So... this weekend, I also attempted to buy some bras at JCP in town; I had to return a few items that I had purchased from them online, so I after that was taken care of, I loaded up my left arm with all sorts of crap to try on. I found camouflage skinny jeans (size 13! wearing them as I type, but like Holy Cow, when's the last time I was a size 13?) and a few $1.97 items. Anyhow, I grabbed bras because I haven't shopped for them in awhile; for some reason, all their 36Ds were large on me. Some in the cup & some around & some both ways. I chalked it up to the brands they carry because Kohl's is where the "reliable" brands are to me. In fact, I just spent a truckload of cash at Kohl's online last night. I like their bra brands, and they had a lot on clearance ($10 bras! Then 25% off on top of that?!). Plus, I got the nephew & nieces some things as well. Kill two or three or four Christmas birds with one credit card. Duh.

Chapter 18: January 2014 (Ten Months Post-Op).

So, I ended the year by taking a trip to the ER. Bonus: My deductible has been blown to shit by this surgery, so I may only have to worry about paying the $50 ER co-pay.

Here's the story:
I get up like normal on Tuesday (December 31), and I think I hopped on the stationary bike for a good twenty minutes before baking some cupcakes for a party I was going to attend that night. The shortened version of the backstory is that my bf's Plan A (although, yes, these plans were not set in stone, as he's mentioned a gazillion times) included him heading to his parents' house Monday night and then ice-fishing with his dad or brother New Year's Eve, etc. Long story short, I wasn't part of his "possible" Plan A, so I made my own plans with friends because I like to act like a high school girl and get all pissy once in awhile.

But, really, think about it: Does high school ever end? Isn't there a song that states it never is over? C'mon.

Anyhow, I make cupcakes, he wakes up... we are not super chatty with one another based on the NYE Plans we've made, etc. I think I ended up on the couch relaxing once the cupcakes came out out of the oven. My plan was to rest and do very little while they cooled off, then after frosting all 24 chocolate-pumpkin cupcakes, I'd shower and get prepped for the party. I was supposed to head to Steph's house – she's a new part-timer at the college, and I have already met up with her at a Bison Hockey game in town – around 6:30/7pm. I had outfits planned out in my little head (she wanted people to wear red) and everything like that.

Well, while I'm sitting or lying on the couch, I notice that the sunlight coming in our south windows is almost in my eyes, and it's pretty strong – even for December winter sunlight. At one point, I think I look right into the damn light, and it causes my eyesight to get weird on me. The left side of my eyesight is blurry with stars, and it's similar to the feeling I've had before I'm about to faint.

I get up, as the boyfriend is outside and I figure I should tell him maybe... well, I just walk around and try to regain normal eyesight. I close the curtains a bit more, and as I sit down to rest again, my left fingers get numb and tingly... then the left side of my mouth and tongue do, too. I kind of freak out in my head because of the whole "left side only" thing, and wonder if I could be having a mini-stroke at my age.

It's about 1pm when all of this occurred, and I go outside to find the bf and ask him if these symptoms mean anything. He shrugs and says he doesn't know, but asks if I want to go see a doctor. I decline, and come back in the house still clenching my left hand to try to regain feeling in it. Slowly, maybe within 15 minutes, everything's back to normal with my face and eyes and fingers, but a massive headache over my eyes shows up. Yay?!

I go online on my iPad, look on Webmd, and see that these symptoms are typical of migraines. I've never had one, so I go to Facebook and ask my friends what tips they have for migraines as I know many people who get them all the time.

My friend Cheryl texts me, probably after seeing the Facebook status, and she tells me that if I've never had a migraine, I should see a doctor. I go upstairs to my bedroom after lying on the couch for possibly 30min; I had taken ibuprophen and put a damp, cool cloth on my melon. The pain was still there, and intense at times. I start to think that it's worse, definitely, than any headache I've had even after a night of drinking.

So, while upstairs, I lie on our bed and call the clinic. The docs there are all booked, but the lady transfers me to the Phone Nurse or whatever you call it. I stay on hold for 15 minutes. No joke. When I talk to her, she is concerned about the numbing sensations I had, and says I should head to the ER. I naively ask if you can just show up at the ER, and she says yes. I start to get really worried at this point, and a teary-eyed me goes downstairs to ask the bf to take me to the ER.

Once we're out there, he hangs out in the waiting room, and I wait and wait and wait... I think we got out there around 2pm and didn't leave until 7pm. It was fairly dead from what I could tell, but what's the rush when a brain's involved, right? Right. I think there were two other trauma patients in the timespan that I was there, so obviously they should be seen first. I just looked like a silly girl with headache, I suppose.

After giving two people all sorts of information and paying my effen co-pay, a doctor sees me.

He thinks it's my electrolytes (and I think instantly of the ladies in my FB fitness group who drink gallons of water before 8am everyday), and I think to myself that I doubt all this is from dehydration. My brain wants to get back at me. I did some crazy kettle bell workout on Monday that made me really dizzy... plus, I've gotten healthy this year; of course karma would pay me back with a stroke or aneurysm, right? I got really pessimistic at times sitting there waiting!

They do blood work, my mom tells my dad to come out there because she's freaking out (yet, she didn't come out?), I'm conversing with Cheryl via text messages and others on FB (updating them really)... I take a pregnancy test before the first CT scan and then wait around some more. At some point, after the first scan, I go out to find my bf and he and my dad are chilling in the waiting room. They seem happy to see me, and are glad I'm not in a wheelchair.

Before my dad and bf come into the room, the nurse shoots my hip with some liquid Motrin? The doctor comes in eventually to tell us about the scan. It looks fine, he says, and they can do a CT-A which uses dye, but it's up to me, etc. etc. I shrug and don't know what to request. I'm no hypochondriac, so if it's nothing, it's nothing. He says he'll get my discharge papers, and that'll be that.

A few minutes later though, he pops in to say he can call up to Sandford in Fargo and have a neurologist view the scan for a second opinion. We say, yes. What's a few more hours of waiting? He does so, and we chat amongst ourselves. I think I lie down for a bit at one point, and my bf turns off one set of lights. My headache, and it's power, go in & out. It's always there – very pressurized above my eyeballs – but with every moment that it feels like it's leaving, it shows back up. Yay. I notice that the lights in the hospital are not as annoying to my eyeballs as they once were. I wore sunglasses to the ER, and that was a great idea because the snow and light outside would've probably made my brains blow through the front of my skull.

The neurologist, a female, says to check for aneurysms with a CT-A scan. I say why not. It's the last day of the year! Perfect timing?! They prep me for that with an IV and ask if I'm allergic to iodine. As the scan wraps up, and that dye is moving through me, my stomach feels funky as does my nether regions. I feel, for a split second, as if I am about to pee myself and barf. The technician says that that is normal. Oh yay?!

After the second scan, I get some dinner (or maybe it was before the second scan? – it's all a blur even two days later) because I've only eaten breakfast that day (the bf is quick to point this out to the nurses and doctors; he definitely doesn't want me to fall apart). The second scan is clean. So, it's not a migraine or a stroke or an aneurysm. Huh. My bloodwork was normal, my scan is normal; it's all a fluke, BUT he says if it happens again anytime soon, I had better get up to Fargo to get an MRI. Awesome, I think, awesome.

Once we're at home, and I've realized my NYE plans were for nothing, I am pooped out. We start watching Happy Ending reruns and order pizza. It ended up being a quiet night, and I'm okay with that. I couldn't imagine drinking after all that anyhow, and the day exhausted me. I did get my kiss and midnight, and I didn't wake up hungover.

I did wake up and experience – rarely – moments when I thought I had taken cold meds. That weird light-headed feeling when I would bend down to grab something or move my head too quickly. But today, this morning, already I feel more like me.

Pre-Pink concert, Alisa and I talk about tampons.

Me: "I can not wait to have a drink and take out my tampon. It's like half-in right now, and that's really pissing me off."

One of us mentions how horrible it feels when the lady bits are semi-dry, and you have to take a tampon out of that semi-desert-like region. It always makes me cringe.

Also, and I hate to admit this, we were trying to find a bar to get a drink at before the concert. Long story short, we got fed up with the pubs around the Fargodome, and so I threw a baby bottle of vodka into my already opened Diet Coke can. First time for everything.

Yeah. Shame, shame, shame, I know my name.

After my first sip, I say: "I should do this more often."
Alisa laughs hard and says: "Yeah, if only it weren't illegal!"

The horrible wind conditions outside today (and my low to no visibility drive yesterday morning to take my bug into the shop) make me think of the crappy conditions my honey drove me up in for my post-op appointments last spring. I think there were at least two or three appointments that landed on very cruddy weather days. He was a trooper about it. And now, with his new job in Fargo, I'm worried about his commute home tonight as well as his drive up there tomorrow morning. We're supposed to get blizzard-like weather. Ugh. I know worrying doesn't help anything, but sometimes, that's all I got.

A snow day was called for tomorrow as I'm Facebook-messaging some friends from campus. They all want to meet up for a drink or two. I say, "Well, what's the verdict; do I have to put on a real bra?"

It's nice knowing I could live in a sports bra right now, and unless you really stared at my chest, you'd never notice the mono-boob. Or uni-boob?

Before bedtime, I read in my ELLE magazine about a book that has been written regarding all the writers who drank and how it helped them. I think aloud, "I should do that more often."

Sometimes, when I get really stressed out, I'll remind myself of this little visual I have of how the world began and will end.

It's all darkness. Nothingness. And then we pop out of nowhere. Stars, moon, the earth, and humans. People are born, animals evolve, plants grow and die. Then, suddenly, just as easily as it began, it's all darkness again. It doesn't matter, in my little daydream visual, how it all begins or ends. All that it tells me is that we don't matter. Nothing exists later on. I will turn to dust, and so will my friends and family. This whole idea stresses a lot of people out, but it calms me. It really does, and I know that makes me odd.

It's like, nothing matters. When I have a fight with my partner-in-crime, it feels like it matters, and I want to analyze it, but I need to let it go. I need to enjoy every moment; it's not going to be my moment or my earth or my life for a very long time.

Another thing that freaks people out is dying. I am oddly okay with the concept. I wasn't, for a long time, because I didn't feel accomplished in the ways I wanted to be accomplished. But now, I could go at any time, and I don't think – in my last breaths – I would feel much regret. Others might say, "Oh, she didn't get married; she didn't have children; she didn't x, y, or z," but those thoughts are THEIR thoughts. Not mine.

There is so much relief in just realizing that you don't have to apologize for who you are.

For example, I spoke my mind last night – in a fairly non-hostile way – to my boyfriend, and it wasn't a nice thing to say. It wasn't, but it was a fact for me. I was open with him on what I thought about something he had said, and I think I semi-upset him. He said later that he just really wanted us to have nice things, and I started – again – to think about how he likes quality items & I wish he wanted quality experiences just as much (cut to our argument about going to the goddamn Twins game this summer), but we are different creatures. For sure.

We shouldn't always have to apologize for our different outlooks on life. And I don't need to say I'm sorry for a fact that came out of my mouth. It was possibly too honest, but this is a characteristic of me he seems to like most of the time.

Speaking of time, we've been having flirty little sessions since sometime last week. For about a week there, or more, he was distant and probably just tired. For a second last night, after I said what I said, I thought, "Oh great, I've ruined the nice goofyness we've been having," but I don't think a person should constantly worry about that.

Since this damn book is about boobs & body issues, I suppose I should comment on those things real quick-like. The chest has been shrinking... or my bras are suddenly larger than normal. The breasts also feel like they have small rocks in them; I wonder if they will ever go away.

My weight loss – now around the 34lb range – stalled out in early December. I consulted many friends in person and online, and they figured I wasn't eating enough. So, I reconfigured my stats in the MFP (myfitnesspal) app I use; as of last Friday, I was down almost two pounds. So, yes, kids, sometimes you do need to eat more to lose weight. Weird bodies!

January 22, 2014:

You would think that maybe a person who has lost 30+ pounds would be more cold in the winter times, but I haven't noticed any change in how warm I can get... even with wind chills and blizzard warnings. Either that is just how my body is, or I have gained muscle and muscle insulates us better? I think I should scientifically just go with the former idea on that. Yep.

I had a Wildtree Taste-testing party last night, and I was able to get some things off my mind with the ladies. Long story short, my epiphany was that I give myself enough guilt trips, and that that is the reason I detest (or hate – if I'm feeling harsh) when others attempt to give me guilt trips. My mom, present at the party, has been know to be the Guilt Trip Queen, but she pointed out instead that she tends to give homework. That is her new thing to do: "Hey, you look un-busy; how about you do x, y, and z for me." Ugh. Moms. Sheesh.

January 28, 2014:

Well, I spent most of the night pooping and pooping and pooping. I think I had a reaction to my own goddamn birthday cake; is that possible?

And then there's this hot mess of a former student who attempted to argue with me on Facebook last night, too.

Positive Sidenote: I didn't get sick around or on my birthday this year. Last year, I had influenza and the two years before that (or three?) I got stupid strep throat. Ugh.

Chapter 19: February 2014 (Eleven Months Post-Op.)

February 5, 2014:

At water aerobics, the ladies and I discuss fitness tips, etc. A few know now that I've lost a bit of weight – these are ladies who've never met me before – and that I had a reduction first which was the catalyst. One particular woman, who I know on campus, asked me what I used to lose weight, and I said, "I started using that app My Fitness Pal and biking more this summer." Her response was that she didn't have time to log her food like that. She might've even said, "Who has time to do that!" and I thought, "Well, obviously I did so you might've just put me down for not being 'busy enough' and you also seem to not care enough about your own health to keep a food journal. It doesn't take that long, and I typically eat the same things everyday."

February 7, 2014:

I got my second (or maybe third) request regarding my surgery tonight. I think I told the extremely shortened, and extremely positive version, but the person who asked seemed genuinely interested.

After talking to her that night, and to my other tipsy friends from campus, I mentioned again aloud that I wanted to write my own erotica – my own <u>Fifty Shades of Grey</u>. They encouraged me, and we started talking about other books that need to be written.

February 8, 2014:

My campus pals putzed out on going dancing. I probably drank the most last night, and THEY are the ones who want to stay in. Ugh. Oh well. I'm going to start to write that damn erotica book that's in my head. This book about boobs will be completed soon, and I'll obviously need a new project.

I really wanted to go dancing to show off this new small body I have. That's all.

I named the main character in my erotica book, Georgia. And then what kinds of license plates do I see yesterday while in Fargo (North Dakota!)!? Georgia plates. It's a sign!

Deleting myself from a group has never felt so fucking awesome!

Yesterday, and even before then, the secret fitness group I was a part of on Facebook was really getting on my nerves. When I first got invited to the group, I was excited. Within a few days, I noticed that they were kind of a one-tune crew. Or at least it felt that way. Running + gallons of water + tracking food. I was reluctant, but I wrote on there about tracking and biking and trying to guzzle water...

Every so often, I would post about my weight-loss. I would also partake in certain challenges that the group had. I think during one of the challenges I lost 10lbs (October?), but things came to their breaking point recently when I mentioned how I was reading this book – <u>Why We Get Fat</u> by Gary Taubes. He's a scientific journalist, and the amount of studies he read was nuts. I was sucked into the studies he read, the history he provided (those damn German doctors probably had it right – eat meat! – but then World War II made us hate German anything), and the idea that we're really just a nation addicted to sugar. We're active, we eat organic, we do this and we do that and yet we're all fucking obese?! What the hell! Hey, maybe it's not our activity or how much we eat; what if it is about WHAT we are eating?

Okay, so obviously, I liked his message. It's not an easy fix though because even though I love protein, I am "addicted" in some sense to eating carbs and not the good ones at times.

Anyhow, I bring up the book in this secret fitness group. A few join me in discussing it all. I even posted pictures of the book's "diet" at the end (from Duke's Medical University or something like that), but by the next day, the pictures were gone and message from the "new" leader was on there about how that group was not about "fad" diets. She had even posted some new food pyramid. I was pissed. There are vegans and vegetarians in the group who obviously don't eat certain things on the pyramid, yet my idea of lowering one's carb intake is a "fad." Whatever.

So, yeah, I left a "thanks for everything" note on the previous leader's post about all of us respecting each other, and deleted myself.

And I started my own damn group. The Lean, Mean, Awesome Machine group. We swear and appreciate all ideas; only pills seem like fads to us...

I feel like a water-loving, 5K-doing monkey jumped off my back.

February 25, 2014:

So, I called in sick Friday morning because I felt about 138.6-years-old when I woke up. And I could not breath out of my nostrils (that is such a pet peeve of mine!). I thought, "Well, I haven't been sick for over a year." And it's true. On my birthday in 2013, I had some sort of influenza. I should clarify that I was pretty much over it by the time my birthday rolled on in.

After that, I remember my surgeon stressing how I could not get ill in the months leading up to my surgery. She wouldn't operate on me if I came in with a cold or whatever. So, I remember eating my vitamins and trying to be good to myself all those weeks.

It's crazy that this coming Saturday will be my one year anniversary of chopping off the boobies. It's so strange. Sometimes, it feels like a year, and sometimes it feels like it was just yesterday.

I called in sick yesterday, too, because the weekend didn't quite heal me. I also ended up sleeping on the twin long bed in the office because my bf was snoring. I actually like all the beds in our house (soft or hard), and I zonked right out when I moved to that bed. However, when I woke up on my stomach... and that bed is harder than our master bed... I could feel my back and chest respond. The lumps that still exist in my chest were hard and almost felt pissed off. Like, "What the fuck is wrong with you woman? You can't sleep on us ON a HARD bed. Get a brain."

February 28, 2014:

Well, a year ago today, I was uber nervous. The kind of nervousness that causes nausea and a low appetite.

This morning, I woke up before my alarm. Fairly rested. I saw a text from the bf; he got to the casino hotel last night safely & commented on the smokiness of the place.

I took "a year later" photos... I remember last year wondering if I should take a "before" pic, and I'm glad I did. Even though I now have that big-boobied picture on all my Apple devices (leads to interesting situations!), I'm glad I have a "before." Same goes for the "before" I took in June previous to losing the weight I've lost.

Last night, I attempted to have a "Save the Boobies: A Year Later" party. It ended up being a small group, but festive one. My officemate came out for a beer, as did another English colleague. The last two standing, until about 8pm, were me and my newest friend Dawn. I say new friend because just in the last six months, we've become buddies, and I adore her. Anyhow, during our conversation, I noticed that leftie was being an asshole again, and I told her about the book title possibilities. "I am probably going to call it <u>Big-Boobed Bridesmaid</u>, but it could also be called <u>Leftie is An Asshole</u>." She giggled.

I think a guy could write a book with the same title, really. And that makes it even more versatile!

Today, I have one class, then I need to grade only a half of a ton of shit before I check my parents' house, eat lunch, and head to Leadership Academy. I finished the goddamn book (<u>The Speed of Trust</u>) for that group; it wasn't horrible – like Shakespeare – but it just wasn't interesting. It was kind of like reading Emerson (although Ralph Waldo was a genius)... I recall Steve Ward saying, "Emerson writes a bunch of b.s. and then there will be a nugget of awesomeness." Okay, that's a paraphrasing! But still. This Stephen Covey (his dad was the genius behind "The Seven Things Highly Effective People Do" or some title like that) is like that; and then he went and named HIS son Stephen (his dad's name was Stephen). Why does that bug me? Or when people name their kids all with the same letter? Why does that bug me, too?

Tonight, we have a "safety meeting." Then, I'd kind of like to go dancing. A band, named Helena Handbasket, is in town. At first, I thought their name was Helena Highwater. Love that name. Why am I talking about names today. Wake up, woman!

Oh, how's this for random: You know how you typically have one (or more?) pores that produce the same annoying chin hairs? Same spot every time? Yeah, that's happening with leftie. There is a spot under the nipple that continually creates the same little dark brown hair. Go the fuck away, weirdo hair?! BUT then again, I remember reading that when the hairs start to grow around and in the incision areas, that means healing has started big time. I just wish they would all be WHITE or CLEAR hairs, for crying out loud. That's not too much to ask.

While I'm asking, I'd like stretch marks to be in different designs. Plaid. Pok-a-dotted. Yeah. Somebody get on that!

Chapter 20: March 2014 (One Year Post-Op).

March 3, 2014:

I just shared my before/after pic with my happy little fitness group (of all women) on Facebook, so perhaps I should share it here too. I mean, it visually explains a lot.

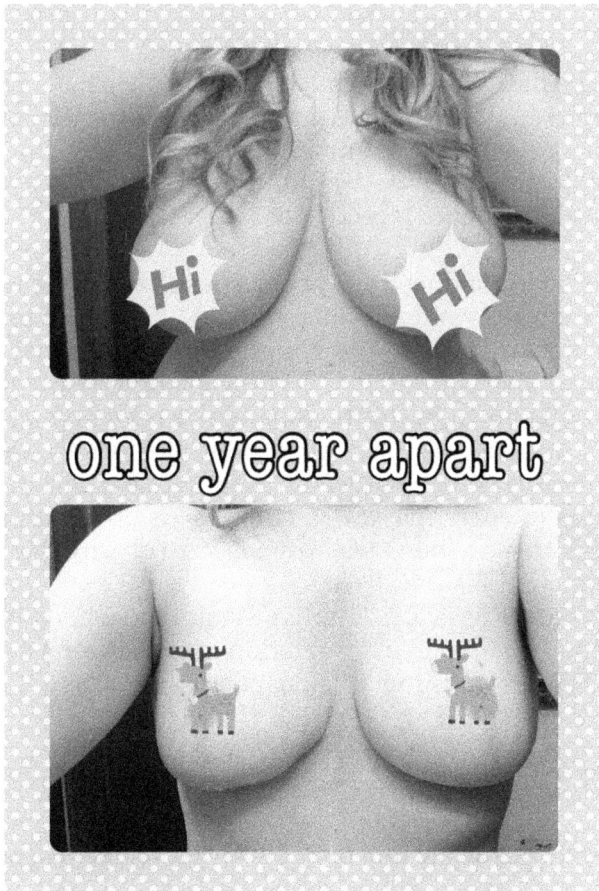

I don't know why I used the stickers I used, but they are cute and humorous. You can barely see my scars in the bottom pic under the reindeer. They have definitely faded from a darker pink (in December) to now.

I really need to finish up this book. And yet, I find myself working on other things. For example, today, I wrote a small essay (seriously small = 150 words) for a bicycling magazine contest. They want parodies of one of their bloggers; the person with the best parody wins a bike listed in the magazine's most recent "Buyer's Guide" up to $4999. Holy crap, right?

If I win that kind of bike, I would feel so very, very, very badass. VERY.

I finished up the day with two drinks with KJ. We chatted about quite a few topics, and the one we ended on was what her plan is for her chest. She's got a different situation than I do with the lurking cancer, but I told her to not do shit for that first week and that if she has a mini-breakdown like I did, it's okay.

I told her to ask a lot of questions at her consultation because I didn't. I didn't know I wouldn't have drains, I didn't ask to see the surgeon's before and after shots, I didn't know my stitches would be dissolvable, etc. I also commented on how I should really try to get all these questions down in this book, and she said, "It's okay. You can't do it all." And honestly, every region in this country, every surgeon who performs these procedures might do it differently. It's too much for me to encompass; I can only focus on my journey. That's what this freakin' book was supposed to do anyhow.

This book's possible message: "Hi. I'm Sybil. I have body image issues. So, I finally had a breast reduction at the age of 36 and lost 30+ pounds. There is nothing about cancer in here. Yep. Um, I hope you enjoy reading it!?"

I weighed myself yesterday morning because I felt scrawny when I got up.

164. Up almost three pounds? What the hell? Then I stopped my freak out session, mid-swear word, and reminded myself that it could be added muscle, it could be a basic fluctuation because I'm supposed to get my period, or it could be that THAT fucking number doesn't matter!

Cut to this morning... my typical weigh-in day (for the last few months anyhow), I jump on the scale around 6am after feeding Little Miss Stare-At-You-While-You're-Sleeping kitty cat Sushi.

162. Only up .2 from last week? Okay. Step on it again. Same number. Ditto for the third try. Since our floors are not level (who has a home in the Red River Valley that DOES have level floors? Oh, you do? Good job. You win!), I always step on the damn thing three times.

Right before I know my bf's alarm is about to go off, 6:15am, I realize I have to poop (drinking any amount of Grey Goose does this to me). I head downstairs to do so; afterwards, I figure I might as well pop back on the scale to see if I got rid of some actual weight. The scale decides to bounce back and forth from 164 to 159 and then to 162 and back to 159. I sigh, groan, and shook my head.

I want to ask the scale: What the fuck is your problem? Can you make up your fucking mind please?

At least it didn't jump up to 170 and down to 150. Long story short, I might need to invest in a new scale or put the scale in a location where it can be horizontal the whole time. I doubt me putting it vertical (to fit in between the toilet and cabinet) is causing it to mis-calibrate or whatever, but jeezus martha and mary.

I put 162 into my MFP (myfitnesspal) and crawled back into bed for a few more semi-relaxing minutes.

March 6, 2014:

I appreciate advice. I really, truly do. But when I get unsolicited advice, especially when I didn't accidentally (yep, I've accidentally done it) ask for it, I zone it out. Last night, at my water class, the instructor came over to me while I was in the range of her husband (in the water) and told him I was training for a Half Marathon and a triathlon.

Here's the back story: A few weeks back, I might have asked her what she thought of me taking just one class after Spring Break because I'm currently swimming three times a week. We chatted about it, and came up with me taking just the Wednesday night class, etc. So, when she asked him about it, I thought, "Whoa, wait a minute. I have my training schedule figured out. And why is she asking him to help me? Do I look that clueless?" She misinforms him that I'll be taking three water classes again (no, we already discussed that), so his first idea is that I should take water aerobics classes Monday, Tuesday, Wednesday, and run the other four days of the week. Immediately, I'm thinking, "Dude, you've obviously never trained for one of these. I've researched a few different schedules online, and a person needs rest days and long run days and strength-training days, etc." I laugh at his first idea and tell him that I have a schedule, and that it has two rest days built in because after a long run it's practically required. He says that I should definitely be in the water on my rest days, though, because I can stretch better. While this is true, that isn't always possible with my schedule and with the pool's schedule. Doesn't he get that? And his idea of me swimming MTW wouldn't work either because she doesn't have a class on Mondays.

Anyhow, he launches into how important it is that I stretch the day after my longest run. And I should do that after my actual Half, too. I'm nodding through the whole ordeal, remembering how I did that when I trained before. He's telling me stuff I know. I always detest those kinds of conversations – not because they are annoying, but because they are wasted energy. It's sad how often I have to ponder: "Do I look stupid? Do I appear to not know stuff?"

And then this lead me to thinking about how only I know my body. I know how I need to train, how I need to lose weight, how I need to gain muscle. My body is different than anyone else's, and how I think about my body is different than everyone else, too. This journey has DEFINITELY taught me that much. So, I let him talk; in my head, I'm thinking – stubbornly almost – that I have it mostly figured out.

Halfway into the class, he looks upset to me, and somehow I feel badly that I didn't give him my full attention. Granted, I didn't ASK for the information, but still. I don't know him, and he doesn't know me. So, during a lull, I ask if he knows anyone who has done a triathlon. He shouts to his wife leading the class & they throw a name at me. I don't know the person. I tell him that I have the biking down and the running, but I'm wondering how to train for the water. He tells me to take one of his wife's other classes, and I start to think, "No, dude, I mean, do people train in a lake for this? Do they try to camp out at a lake and do all three in one day to train or something crazy like that?" I've taken swimming lessons; I know how to do the American crawl. Sure, her class might make me faster, but I'm not really concerned about that... this will be my first Sprint Triathlon in August, and I just want to complete the damn thing.

I'm sure they meant well. I might just have to keep some of my training ideas to myself?

March 11, 2014:

While at a meeting on campus just now, I saw this guy, who retired awhile back, walk by the classroom we were meeting in. Everyone on campus likes the guy; my friend Dawn even said how he gushed over his recent bride, etc. Well, what sucks about knowing him for me, because apparently he's a "really nice guy," is that my first impression of him is not a good one.

He walked into my office a few years back to talk to me about some grant thing, and when I stood up to shake his hand, he looked directly at my chest. Yep. And that's all I remember. And it wasn't like they were "on display."

So, he probably is a "nice guy," but that moment is ingrained in my melon.

So yeah... reliving what happened to me this past year hasn't been as easy as I thought it would be. As I edit and re-read, I realize how tortured I was. About my body, about my life and where it was/is headed,... about him & I. This is harder to do than I thought, and I think it's going to take me longer because it's not as much "fun" to read the second time around.

It's amazing how much someone can "grow" in a year. Or shrink, for that matter.

And... I really want to get this completed before KJ has her surgery, so she can read it while she recovers.

I told her yesterday evening that I've lightened some of the harsh words I had originally used to describe some situations and some people. I said, "This book isn't about throwing anyone under a bus; it's geared at people like her (or insert anyone who has asked me about it) who want to know what I went through."

Last night – perfect timing! – I finished Sloane Crosley's book, <u>How Did You Get This Number</u>. She's hilarious, for one, but the best part was the final paragraph. I'm definitely using it in my conclusion.

An image pops up in my Facebook newsfeed. "Don't be ashamed of your story; it will inspire others."

I went for a 5 mile run on Saturday, and while I felt rather slow (because of the goddamn wind), I noticed that when I constantly correct my posture while running, I run better. I still tend to slouch, but oh well. I'll keep working on it.

Our mom turned 60 last week. So, we had a sort of "surprise" birthday party Saturday night for her. I think she enjoyed herself, and what I noticed about myself was that I wasn't worried about taking photos. It was possibly the first time I was at a large gathering not worrying about how I looked to people – how I'd look in photos – I wasn't hunching a lot to make my chest appear smaller or anything. Honestly, I think I was the most worried about my butt crack because I was squatting down a lot to talk to our niece Audrey.

March 31, 2014:

During my 3pm class, a huge bunch of people came into the room clapping and cheering... I won one of four Excellence in Teaching Awards for this year. I guess forty-six teachers got nominated, and the committee chose me as one of the best four for this year. I'm still shocked & my heart is beating relatively quickly!

I think I was nominated last year and the year before that. Students do the nominating & then a particular committee gets together to narrow down the choices to four. I think that's how it works. Anyhow, what a cool Monday it ended up to be!

The only thing I thought when viewing the photos a few colleagues took after = I need a haircut and some highlights. I didn't have anything negative to say about my body or chest. Yay!

Chapter 21: April 2014.

I got up really late this morning, and he looked concerned when I came down the stairs in my running gear. "You were pretty tired, huh?" I nodded. "You going for a run?" I nodded again and said, "Yeah, I gotta get a long one in."

When I returned, he had made some pork stir-fry. He offered me some and seemed shocked or impressed that I had run 6-7 miles.

We got groceries later on, and even hit Wallymart to see if they had pantries – he wants one in the basement. I think I mentioned that my bike computer wasn't working. And he fixed it.

So, yesterday, I woke up with a massive pain in my left eye... it was watering, too; my head also had a major ache to it – almost a migraine feeling. I called in sick to campus and tried to sleep it all off.

That didn't work.
I called into the clinic for an appointment. They say they can get me in right away. I drive there in a blur of sensitive eyeballs and tears.

The eye doctor, after I totally complete the eye chart in my 20/20 awesomeness, says I have an inflamed cornea in my left eye. Ugh. She prescribes steroid drops, wants me to check in on Wednesday to see if it's getting better, and tells me to hang out in a dark area for 24hours.

I get home and eat lunch and check email and nap, etc. in our dark master bedroom, with my sunglasses on.

Jan gets home, calls me Bob Costas, and I catch him up on the whole thing. I head back upstairs to our bedroom, and he comes up later to shower. We chat a bit about what happened at his workplace, and then he heads downstairs to watch TV and make dinner.

I decide to try to spice things up, and I put on this red bikini I bought awhile back from ASOS.com. I bring some garbage downstairs, and he seems a wee bit shocked that I'm in a bikini. He asks about a rash near my neck & asks me if I'm cold. These are not really the reactions I was going for.

I head back upstairs. I change into my fitted yoga capri pants and a tee and watch more TV. I then decide to go back downstairs and ask him about a previous idea I had (last Friday?). The "date night" idea.

He says he's up for it. "Let's do it on Friday." Now, as I reflect back on the hours of arguing that followed this, I can see that he was trying to "push my buttons" as he tends to do. He knows I go out with my girlfriends on Fridays. Maybe he's jealous of this, maybe he doesn't really care because he gets the house to himself when I'm not there when he gets home, maybe he just knows how to "get me going" down the anger path.

I do tell him that I could make that work because my plans with friends for dancing aren't until later. Suddenly, me making time for a day that he just threw out there (in reflecting again, I see that I should've asked if we could compromise on a day and not just go with his first choice) is me not "taking this idea seriously." It comes to me like this: "If you thought this idea was important, you would make time for it."

Wow. And maybe if he knew it was important to me, he wouldn't use it as a tool to push my buttons with? If he thought it was important, he would also make sure the day was a compromise instead of just a day that he decided upon.

Later, into the arguing of all this, he says he's right. He knows he is. I start to wonder if I am really, truly, with a man who has to be "right" even if it is at the sacrifice of my happiness. He would rather be right than happy. He would rather be right than just have a discussion about things and try to see my perspective.

At the end of February, he had training & a company holiday party to go to near the cities. I had Leadership Academy that Friday, but I wanted to go to the party with him. Before he headed down, I found out – through a discussion while his brother was here – that he was going to travel from the training to Lake of the Woods to ice-fish with his buddies. What if I had mentioned this "date night idea" that week? I didn't know about his plans – as he didn't know about my dancing plans – and I wouldn't have made him decided between me and his friends. I especially wouldn't make him cancel already-made plans. I don't think I ever have.

Anyhow, I think we eventually decided on Saturday evening for a possible date night this week. I had to ask him, after he gave a monologue about his life (it was kind of a pity party; the guy worked at a bar for many years and got to sleep in and fish whenever, so of course things are different this time around – I refuse to believe that this change in his life is completely my fault or my responsibility). I had to ask him like a weak little girl asking out a guy she really likes. He paused for a long time and then said yes.

He proceeded, then, to go downstairs and make a lot of noise. So much noise, I went down to see if he was okay.

I can't recall the movie this line comes from, but: "Can I have a normal boyfriend, please?"

Or, I guess I could quote a blogger friend of mine from way, way back in the day, "Life is not all about 'the boy.'" Duh. Yep. For sure.

April 9, 2014:

We didn't speak yesterday.

I woke up in the middle of the night because Sushi was clawing at the office door (damn thing locked herself in there or rather I didn't know she was in there when I closed the door last night); I opened it and she ran out and then I peed. When I came back to bed, his big dumb leg was over the top of the covers. I tugged on them, "Honey, your leg. Honey..." Ugh.

I grabbed my pillow and phone and went into the upstairs den to sleep. When I heard his alarm go off this morning, I got up and went back into our bedroom. He made sure to close the dresser drawers loudly. I thought, "Real mature. After all those years of me tippy-toeing around your apt when you were a bartender, you are going to be rude this morning. Well, do not worry; I won't be able to go back to sleep for 45 more minutes. Have no fear, nimrod."

Ugh. Meanwhile, my left eyeball aches and my left breast continues to be the one with the phantom lumpy parts. But don't worry, everyone, I won't have a pity party.

April 10, 2014:

So, the silence was broken last night. I was a bit shocked that he decided to talk to me. We talked about why I slept in the den the last two nights (I made him laugh – one thing I do like to do – about his fucking toes and how when he's sleeping on his belly, they dig into the bed like they are digging their way to China).

And then we talked about the gas bill – I know, very romantic! – but it was a regular couple-y conversation that somehow lead to me saying, "YOLO," which made me feel like I was an annoying hipster. That led to a conversation about reincarnation because, you know, if you are a person who says that acronym YET has Buddha shit in your office, you are probably being contradictory. Which is totally possible. I'll admit that I'm wrong, that I'm a hypocrite, that I say stupid shit... how many people can just admit that?

Anyhow, in the process of this conversation, I changed from a regular bra to a sports bra for sleeping in (I bought almost a million of these medium support/thin sports bras to wear post-surgery, and they are perfect for sleeping in)... in front of him. I'm assuming he checked out the little ladies on my chest. I'm pretty sure rightie was nipping out, so I hope he appreciated the little nudie show. I know I appreciate gazing at his ass when he comes out of the shower.

I ended up zonking out only to wake up around 5am to him digging again and then the basic restless leg syndrome laundry list: frog legs while he lays on his back, digging to China while on his belly, putting his legs over the covers when he's on his side.

We are polar opposites in many ways, and sleeping is just one of them. I am a light sleeper – like my Dad – and I just need to curl up on my side, and I'm good.

He can sleep through Sushi barfing, a hail storm, and probably World War 3.

Not like I need more reasons to probably not have children, but these sleeping issues might be reasons 46, 47, and 48. Maybe.

April 23, 2014:

I was messaging on Facebook last night with a girl who I know through the boyfriend (it's his buddy's wife). She was at the starting line when I ran my first Half a few years back. She ran with me for about a block and then took off, being one of those less-than-10-minute miler people.

Anyhow, she isn't able to run the Half due to a leg issue, and I feel for her. She did a lot of training, and now she's walking the 5K and going to try to run the 10K Saturday morning. I told her how I hope I'm faster based on the weight loss and the reduction.

It's strange to me that it has already been over a year since the surgery. When I told her, I thought, "I hope she doesn't think I mean this last March, but like LAST March."

Thus far, I have noticed that my chest gets sore just like my legs. I think I've noticed the phantom lumps – along with a "sore muscle feeling" – the most after sleeping and running. As of right now, as I sit here in my office, I don't have any weird feelings in them. It's nice to know how far I have come emotionally, mentally, and physically.

Speaking of physically, I've been in full-training mode for the Half. I ran a long eight miles on Easter Sunday (before I headed up to Fargo to see Hilary and Jed and Emmett and a bunch of other crazies), and a crappy four miles yesterday. The pinched nerve I had last week (right hip) went away after the Wednesday massage and water aerobics class only to show up as an overall area of soreness at the top of the hip. Yesterday, the sore parts "moved" to the front of the hip, or basically at the top of the quad. So, I've been walking around like an old man. It's awesome (sarcasm)!

Jane, the new Associate VP on our campus, is a runner and told me to buy a foam roller to massage my muscles with. I found one at Dunham's on Monday in Fergus Falls for $35. It has definitely helped to work those leg muscles of mine that are not exactly used to all this work.

This coming Friday is our campus' Rewards and Recognition Banquet. I'm being honored with one of the four Excellence in Teaching awards, which is just the cherry & frosting & sprinkles on the top of a fucking awesome cupcake of a year. Seriously.

And I had the "unfortunate challenge" of trying to find a dress for the occasion. I put that phrase in quotes because it was FUN to find dresses this time around. My body is easier to FIT into shit. Sure, not everything fits, but this time I'm not thinking, "God DAMN these boobs. Damn them all to hell."

Far left to far right: Size 10 dress, large dress, & a snug size 12. What's even more amazing? That I took pictures and shared them with people to get their thoughts on what to wear. The "big me" would not have done that. At least, I'm pretty sure she wouldn't have shared the image with more than her tight-knit crew.

On an unrelated note, I feel like I should comment on how things are going with Jan. But before that, you need to know about Dr. Dorry. Yesterday, after listening in on Dr. Dorry's second (and last, unfortunately) session in front of the OTA & Pharmacy Tech (etc.) students, I made a shortened version of what I learned on Facebook.

Sybil Priebe
Yesterday · Edited

Session #2 with Dr. Dorry:
1. Control Theory = No one can make me think, feel, or do anything I don't choose to do. And vice versa = You can't make someone else happy. (*We will spend the rest of our lives working on this.)
2. We have unique gifts: introspection, a conscience, an imagination, & the power to take action.
3. Self-confident people learn from experience, surround themselves with healthy people, & have passion AND have passionate hobbies.
4. How I spend my time is a statement of my priorities.
5. Check your language = move away from "I have to" or "I can't" to "I choose to" or "I choose not to"...
6. Resist the "righting reflexes" which make us "should" on people.
7. Emotionally Intelligent people are self-aware, they self-regulate, they have self-motivation, they have empathy, and they have effective relationships.

So, when the boyfriend brought up how we should put the silverware upright in the weird slots of the dishwasher (because that's what the manufacturer made them for, you know), I brought up that I am about as likely to do that as he is to put the toilet lid down every time he uses it.

This lead to quite the humorous argument – they happen, oddly, more than our serious ones (and I realize I should be grateful and not say "oddly," but who has humorous arguments with their significant other after 10+ years?) – about how I think I've heard a saying about a person can "be right or be happy but not both." I concluded with the idea that he likes to be right, so I'll just let him think that forever, so I can be happy.

He then states that he is happy when he's right, and says, "Aren't you happy when you are right with your students?" I frown, "If I am right, like about a policy in my syllabus, that doesn't necessarily make me 'happy happy.' I still feel somewhat badly that I 'got 'em!'."

Around this time, I mumbled (mostly to myself, but he thinks I'm doing it to say something snide behind his back) that I guess I won't be happy or right. Funny enough, I know I am happy. I am happy even when I'm not right. Unlike him, I am okay with knowing that I don't know everything. He's got a "thing" with being right. It could be a dude thing?

I then, of course, brought up my Dr. Dorry lessons of the day. I said that I can't make him happy, and he didn't seem concerned about that. In fact, now when I look back on it, his reaction was like, "Duh, that's not your job." Why do I think it is, then?

I really think #1 is hitting me lately, and when he talked about it yesterday, it hit me again. I had to make me happy. With this body, with this chest, with my body issues. On a daily basis, I am in control of me. Not him, not my students, not the people on campus who love me or hate me. I only control me. In some ways, that's so refreshing, and in other ways, it is so fucking scary. I think that last sentence just summed up life in general, didn't it?

Later, he tried to get me to say he SHOULD (see #6 – don't tell people: "You should do ____.") help me with the dishes, etc. I gave in once, catching what he was up to, and then started to say, "I would appreciate you helping me with the dishes, yes." I can be smart even when I am exhausted.

At some point, we started talking about how we want to put a fence up this summer, and he gave me a list of things he wanted me to take care of (calling a surveyor) because he was going to figure out materials, etc. He said something to the effect that this project will solve 99 of his problems "and a bitch ain't one."

"Do you know that hip-hop song." Yes, dear, yes I do.

And for reference, and as an added bonus, here are my abbreviated notes from Dr. Dorry's first session:

Sybil Priebe
April 15

Traci listed some lessons of her week, and then I realized I wanted to jot down what Dr. Dorry said this morning in a session he gave a lot of our health-based students:
--- What you think about, comes about. [Watch your self-talk.]
--- I will start my day with the attitude of gratitude.
--- When you pray, move your feet.
--- Fake it (happiness) until you make it.
--- Leaders are readers (of books!!).
--- Practice, practice, practice!
--- Successful people are "good" finders; they find good in others (or at least try to).

Lastly, I can not wait to get home after classes today. I slept like crap due to my sore right quad and dreams of a student who I knew had lied to me about writing his own paper... so what I'm getting at is that a big nap is in order before I go to deep water aerobics. Jan wants to grill pork chops and corn tonight (he was really upbeat about it, which I found strange and nice all at once).

April 25, 2014:

Yesterday, I drove up to Fargo to hit up the Penny Sale at Happy Harry's, return a dress to Express, and shop at Savers (one of my favorite secondhand stores) before meeting up with my sister at O'Leary's. We were going to eventually attend a spaghetti feed for the Pride Collective and Community Center.

While at O'Leary's we vented about the humans in our life who piss us off.

But beyond that, we also talked about those women in our lives who lack confidence. They are everywhere. Women who put aside what they want to do, what they think, what they feel for others. There are a lot of moms who do this, but I think it's a woman thing in general. We're almost programmed to be givers and not expect shit in return.

We're programmed to think and do a lot of things, really. And if you're remotely religious, it's worse. Religion tells women to have babies, and that that is pretty much their only goal in life. Hell, even on TV, it's reinforced on reality shows when women are trying to get pregnant. And I know I'm making ENORMOUSLY large generalizations – the size of fucking Texas – but what this whole body image journey taught me was that I was programmed to believe a lot of stuff. And some of that stuff – no, MOST of that stuff – was & is shit. SHIT SHIT SHIT. <Yes.

Programming #1: Be happy with your body "as is" because God gave it to you. Unless you have knee issues or ADHD.

Programming #2: You should want babies, so don't screw around with your body parts making this more difficult to occur (birth control, breast reductions, partying, etc.).

Programming #3: Women should be seen & looked at & admired for their outsides... and not heard because our ideas are silly anyhow.

Programming #4: Nontraditional relationships are weird.

Programming #5: If you want to shrink yourself, you aren't a real feminist because you should just be happy with your body as is.

Programming #6: Everything the media tells you about food and how to lose weight is correct. NOT!

Programming #7: Do not do anything to your body to make your partner become unattracted to it (tattoos, cut hair, breast reduction, tone your ass, be sweaty a lot, etc.).

April 28, 2014:

This weekend was a blast even if I did have some bipolar moments.

On Friday, I had one class – a workday mainly for students but I showed a Jon Stewart clip which I should be doing every Friday! – and then I hit the clinic for my annual check-up. The nurse noticed my weight loss, and she also measured my height as 5'7" (my sisters demand that I am an inch shorter = weirdos).

After that, I went home to veg out a bit. I had a nervous stomach for most of the morning, so I grabbed a small bite to eat and headed up to our master bedroom to fix the digital thingie (I failed) and take a nap. I actually did zonk out for a bit – drooling and everything! – before a call from my sister woke me up. She was going to be a bit late, but it was all good.

I got dressed up in my little black dress, I put some bronzer on my legs, and then I hung out in the bathroom doing my hair and makeup until I needed to drive to my parents' house around 1:45pm. We walked up the alley to the Student Center. We used to do that when we were much younger; the campus once had a bowling alley in the basement of the Student Center, and our dad would take us up there to bowl.

I should've told that story for my speech.

Anyhow, the MC for the banquet was funny, and that was nice because it was the first one my parents had attended with me. It went by quickly, and the teaching awards were last. I was shocked by what my students had said in their nominations – I was engaging and organized and didn't treat them like numbers – so when I walked up to the podium, I was more bewildered than anything. I think I said that I was shocked by their words, that I was sorry for calling them nimrods, and that I was touched.

It was short and funny. It could've been more, and I kind of beat myself up after. I should've said X, I should've said Y. It was a little too much mental torture for such a short occasion, really.

And what really blows is that halfway into my little ditty up there, I looked out into the audience and saw the woman who had told a friend of mine that I didn't deserve the award. I'm paraphrasing because she actually told my friend that she couldn't support a vote for me in the teaching excellence committee... that her advisees thought I wasn't a good teacher, and that she had talked to my boss about how horrible I was.

I wish I would've tuned her out. I wish I would've read the quote I had from Ayn Rand. I wish I would've made a joke using George Carlin. I wish I would've done a lot of other things during that little speech – like told certain people to fuck off – but it is what it is, you know?

I also wondered why I didn't tell my story. How I grew up only blocks south of this campus, how I learned how to ride my bike here, and how when I got let go from my first teaching job at a high school in Minnesota, an older teacher said, "You're on to bigger & better things, kiddo." He was so right, by the way.

At some point, maybe it was on Saturday or yesterday, I thought, "You know, I think I'll have another opportunity to say what I wanted. I think I'll probably win this award again, so I'll just focus on being awesome so that that can happen."

Yeah.

Here are more ideas to add to the Programming List:

Programming #8: When your boyfriend wants you to drop your plans to be with him, you should.

Programming #9: Women's likes and concerns and "guilty pleasures" are lower on the totem pole of cool than men's likes and concerns and "guilty pleasures."

Programming #10: Watch your language and watch his language. When he says, "Do what you want," he's insinuating that typically you do what he wants, and he is now giving permission to do what you want even though you were going to do it anyway.

Chapter 22: May 2014.

Yesterday, we spent a lot of money at places and walked out with nothing. I ordered a sweet-ass red and white and black Trek road bike at Scheels… and after Emmett's first birthday party (my nephew), we ordered a whole truckload – or close to a whole truckload – of fencing from Menards to be delivered/shipped to our house.

Jan had a Menards rebates card from last May, and we wondered aloud why we had one for $60. "Oh, that's when we did the flooring in the upstairs hallway," he said. "Yeah, I was recovering." "Wow, that project is a year old now," he concluded. Crazy how time flies when you're having fun.

As we drove home, we chatted about the project again, – he likes to pick on people who repeat their stories, but he does it! – and I started to think about rules. I think I had the same thoughts roll through my head when I returned from the Easter gathering a few weeks back.

Basically, any "rule" is meant to be broken in some way. We are bombarded with messages that tell us we have to look a certain way to be beautiful; we are bombarded – by society and the media and family and friends – that we have to have an 8 to 5 job with a 401k and a saving account and that we have to pay for cable & internet and that we should have a new car every 5 years.

We are bombarded with the idea that certain things should be done in certain orders: college, marriage, babies, retirement, death. These procedures and rules are just stupid. For one thing, no where in there are the really, really tough things. What I mean by "tough things" are those things the general population will never accomplish.

Yes, I'm talking about things I HAVE completed. A Master's degree, a Half marathon, 90 miles on a bike in one day for the MS Bike Tour, publishing a book (or TWO), been with the same significant other for over a decade, ...

How many people do I know who have accomplished those things? Before the age of 40? And not only can I brag that I've done these things, but I've done them under the constant pressure to do OTHER things. To get married, have kids, buy a NEWER house, buy a NEWER car, and to do less intellectually.

Essentially, what I want my message to be – in addition to "your body is your fucking body & if you want a reduction, just do it" – is that there are no rules for women even if you/they think there are. Do not succumb to peer pressure. Do what YOU want to do.

I am happy. It's a battle in me, almost daily, between the girl voice who has heard what everyone else has told her to want and do and feel, and the woman who is like, "Fuck that shit." They fight in my head a lot, but I'm okay with it. Most of the time.

Also, this goes for "small things," too. If you don't want to shave your legs or arms or armpits, don't. Don't feel badly if you have stubble when you go to the swimming pool. It's not worth the worry. If you want to cut your own hair and color it on your own, go for it. Don't let a stylist tell you they HAVE to do it; don't let them tell you that your split ends are gross – the HAIR on your head IS DEAD.

Lastly, whatever you've been told... rethink it. Make sure it's a belief to you. I did this in college with religion. I didn't believe, for myself, that I had to go to church on Sunday to be good. I went all Thoreau on myself and realized I could talk to a higher power whenever I wanted to.

And now I pray to George Carlin. He listens.

Example: Last night, Jan tells me he's getting a cold sore. I say that I just read that Vaseoline works on those. He says, "If that were true, everyone would know it & that company would make tons of money." I say, "I know! The lady who used to wax me told me how women should just use one-bladed razors on their bikini area. No one does, and they get those red bumps, but I do use those cheap ones & they work just fine. No one wants to believe it because everyone else does the opposite!"

Are we all really good sheep? Shit.

May 6, 2014:

Well, I got my "last run" in this morning before the beastly race on Saturday. I thanked Dana for talking me off many ledges in the last few weeks – the worrywart in me needed to be calmed the fuck down. Numerous times. It's all mental, but what ISN'T mental?

Careers are mental, sex is mental, life is mental, relationships and friendships are mental. It's all exhausting if you accidentally fall into the goo known as mental overload. Or mental overthought. I think that's a new word. You're welcome.

Hell, maybe it's redundant to say "mental overthought" because obviously, if I say, "I overthought that," it's clearly mental. And, with confidence, I can say I overthought my body – what it meant to others, anyhow – a lot. I do less of that. I wear what I want, now. I like this body I've designed.

May 7, 2014:

Last night, I was out with a friend who is going through tough times with her hubby. We vented about men and friends and basically all the humans who piss us off. Then things got fun. Her friend came over to our booth, and they hugged and licked each other's faces... I felt a little out of the loop, but giggled along anyhow. At one point, they started to do a little grabby-grab to each others' boobies. I didn't make much of it, but when we moved to a different booth and I ended up on they same side they were sitting on, I actually panicked for a second thinking, "If they grab mine, will they feel strange?"

That is an uber odd worry, right? I mean, they are lumps of fat like everyone else's, but they have been through some torture. They are – to me – more lumpy than they used to be.

When I got home, I talked to Jan for a wee bit about the fencing. And then I said, "I don't ever want us to keep things from each other," and he pretended to look guilty. He was more intrigued by me saying how much I detest the little kids who had walked by earlier and had to touch the pile of fencing material in the driveway.

Later, in bed and finely tuned on a few cocktails, he and I chatted some more, and I thought he was about to jump my bones, post-shower, but he didn't. I tossed and turned, worried about my left kneecap twisting in the night – it's done that in the past & it hurts worse than fifteen boner toes – and thinking about why we haven't been as active. Sure, we are affection; no, I don't think he'd ever cheat on me... perhaps, I'm demanding something in my head that I THINK I should be demanding. Do I want that kind of intimacy with him more or do I just feel pressure to have us be a couple who "does it weekly"?

I do think he finds me attractive, I don't think having tons of sex makes any couple that much better than any other couple... nor do I really think sex is a barometer for how the relationship is doing IF the people in said relationship are talking. When we aren't talking a lot, I want us to conduct some sexual relations as a band-aid for what's not happening verbally. And that's not good.

I hate thinking so much. It's exhausting. Once again, I can't wait to go home and rest today. I should've really asked my doc about that tiredness I get from time to time; I am not sure if it is all that typical.

May 13, 2014:

I thought his mating call was the loud music he had playing on the radio last night, and so I snuck up there and threw on a red bra & undies.

And that was the ticket.

I win.

May 13, 2014 (Part 2):

So, I ran the 5K on Friday night – kind of by accident – and then ran my second Half Marathon on Saturday. I'm not super sore, but I am still pretty tired. This morning, I could've stayed in bed a lot longer, but I wanted to hit Walmart when the smallest crowd would be there in order to get some essentials and new litter boxes for Sushi.

My sister noticed, at Mile 5, that my running this time around – in comparison to the first Half I did in 2011 when she saw me (and my mom and other sister Robin) at Mile 7 – was different. Different and better. In 2011, she noted that I ran kind of hunched over. Fucking boobs. This time, my posture had improved greatly. She even told Robin before telling me, which means it was something at the forefront of her melon after she saw me Saturday morning.

Not only did my posture improve, but my time did, too. Even with two pee breaks, I busted my time from 2011 by almost 30 minutes! Yep. So, a reduction and weight-loss and some added cross-training (a.k.a. biking & swimming) really helped. Really, really, really.

I saw funny posters and t-shirts, I enjoyed myself, and every time I wanted to focus on the mileage I had yet to accomplish, I hollered at myself to worry about the current mile I was on.

This, I think, is so much like life. I've told a few people this already, but I would be at Mile 5 and think, "I have 8 more of these damn things to go. Jeezus!" followed by, "Calm down. Enjoy this mile, asshole!"

And now as I type, I realize that that is how I feel about this journey. This book. I go back and proofread and think, "Sheesh, I sound like I was depressed. I wasn't me," but I was me. It was me at Mile 5, and I couldn't see what Mile 8 would be like or the finish line. Now I'm at the finish line or beyond it, and things are better. So much better. I may have more confidence than some around me would like me to have, but it's all good.

Time for some coffee & my favorite treat – Atkins' peanut butter cups.

May 14, 2014:

After three drinks with KJ & Cheryl last night, I proceeded to pig out like I haven't pigged out in a long while. It may have been the liquor, but I ate like I was going to die today.

After, while rubbing my Buddha belly, I read on Facebook about a girl who has also been on a weight-loss journey. She mentions her weight now, and it's my weight. She mentions that she's wearing a size 8, and I'm not, and suddenly, I'm comparing myself to someone I don't fucking know on stupid fucking Facebook.

So, I was definitely more upset with myself for the comparison shit than the pigging out part.

And after having lunch with the crew today at El Toro, and sharing what I did to myself last night, I feel better. Today is a new day.

I also shared with the crew that leftie – particularly the nipple – is still quite the asshole. I seriously wonder if I will ever NOT having a sharp pain in that area, and I wonder if it will ever NOT be a hard nipple. It rarely is. It bothers me for about five seconds, and then I think of the alternative that I was dealing with for, you know, 30 plus years, and I calm down and just stop the worry.

Memorial Day:

We went out to my mom's parents' farm. After I saw this picture of me, I thought, she looks like a very fit girl:

Chapter 23: June 2014.

June 3, 2014:

A few weeks ago – May 19 (the Monday I had a dumb meeting, then an awesome sushi-filled department meeting, and then spent $500 on the bug) – I woke up to see that Jan had taken his other truck up to Fargo for work. His Ranger was parked in front of my side of the garage. Yep. So, I had to teach myself how to drive a stick. I sat in the truck – after texting him about where the keys were; he was apologetic – and Youtubed how to drive a stick. Yep, that's me. Laugh all you want. People laugh at my expense a lot. I'm used to it.

So, that night, or the night after, he gave me a "How To Drive a Stick" Lesson. I was nervous, but he was a good teacher. He kept referring to the clutch and gas as ying and yang. I bring up this story because I feel like that is definitely one lesson this whole journey has taught me.

Some days, I worry too much about my chest. About my body. About him and I. About what the future holds and what the past has done to me. But if I stay in the middle, in that curvature that the ying & yang symbol has, I'll be okay.

I can't focus on the past. I don't have the best idea of who that girl was precisely a year ago who wanted to be a size 12. I evolve – we all do – everyday in such teeny ways that when you look back on just a year's worth of change, it can be overwhelming. Proofreading this book was harder, honest to god & Carlin, than writing the damn thing. I feel for the woman I was a year ago. I know she had a lot of power in her thoughts and words, and I know she had confidence, but now I don't have the fears she did. Or at least, I have learned from her to smash those fears into shit. (SNL: "I threw it on the ground!")

I donated almost all the shorts I had from last summer. I am mostly wearing size 12s (last summer, I had 16s). I kept my Levis that will have to be "hemmed" smaller for Moondance.

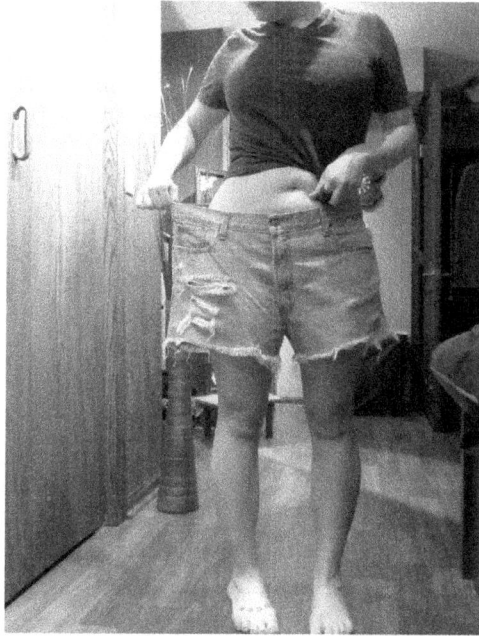

The BIGGEST change on the mental front within the last few months = no more daily torture! What I'm saying is that I no longer have that "baby: yes or no" commercial in my head. Constantly. Constantly. Constantly. It's left me alone. I'll come to that topic when or if I ever have to again.

I am okay with being a 36D. Sure, I asked the surgeon to make me into a C, but it's all good. They are still baby boobies to me.

But it's not all over. Of course.

I'm still learning, of course, and now I feel like I have to learn to let go of my judgments of others. When it comes to chest size and body sizes, it is none of my fucking business what others want to look like. Their body is their body. I have no right to judge it based on its outsides. I really don't. You want a tattoo? Okay. You want pink hair. Cool. You weight 234lbs or 110lbs or 150lbs and/or wear a size XXS or 55" waist or size 12 dress? Fine. I shouldn't be focused in on that stuff or how much weight a person has either. Sure, I've become happier now that I'm leaner, but that doesn't mean everyone else needs or wants that journey as well.

Here's a sad story to go along with these obvious lessons I still have to learn – this is a story I am not proud of. Last Tuesday at sand volleyball, we played our designated team and then one of the teams after us didn't show up. We decided to jump up and play the team who had showed up (they had done the same for us the week before after all). Well, I thought our whole team was playing, and instead, for Game 1 a guy from another team played. SR didn't play, and I gave him crap when he didn't come out to the court for Game 2. I said something like, "Look at him and look at you; you need a little more activity." People's eyes got large, my laughter was stifled – what the fuck did I just say? So, I tried to make up for it, "Hey, I wish someone would've told me the same thing last summer." The person I was making fun of smiled and said, "I have lost some weight." And I nodded.

It was a very shitty situation. I'm hoping to apologize AGAIN for it tonight when I see him. I had texted him the next morning. Tipsy or not, true or not, I had no right to point out anything about his appearance.

Oddly, I am so used to people disliking me (students, mostly) that I don't watch out for those who do like me & try to be better to them than most.

It's not over when it comes to my body either. I have started weight-lifting; I'm hoping to make June all about that. At the end of the month, I am doing my first Run or Dye 5K. July is the Bike MS Tour. August will see my first triathlon, and in September, I'm possibly doing my last Half (or just my third in a long line of them?) with my awesome friend Dana.

June 3, 2014 (Part 2):

So, I decided to watch some things that I had DVR'd last night, and my rib cage felt too tight. Off went the sports bra! In fact, I do that from time to time now; I just take off bras and continue on with whatever I'm doing in the house. I did consider – I forgot to right about this – not wearing a bra to Graduation just to be a little bit of a rebel. And also to see what it felt like, if anyone could tell, etc. They are still fairly perky – which is weird for someone who has always felt like they were headed towards her fucking belly button at too early of an age – and as I type this, I still don't have a bra on.

Rightie is doing that whole "small shooting pains" though. They are small pains, and I can't remember if I had strange little shooting pains when I had larger breasts. In fact, if you are reading this and you have a large chest AND experience shooting pains through them from time to time, will you contact me? For real. Just email me and say, "Yes, Sybil. Little pains of fun through my chesticles weekly" or whatever.

Oddly, on the way up the staircase – which I swear is where one can burn 100 calories going up – I held my chest like I used to hold my "old chest." But they don't move. They don't need my hand-based support. It's still weird after ALL THIS TIME.

June 4, 2014:

It's National Running Day, and I bet before all this happened to me, I would've rolled my eyes at anyone who posted about running or being healthy.

This journey has definitely made me rethink how I take care of myself.

I did a combo workout today, and now I am beat. I biked to our fitness center, did an Arm Day for weight-lifting, and then attended one of 6 water aerobics classes I'll take this summer before biking back home.

I'm now full of tater-tot hotdish – thanks to Jan's leftovers – and sitting, typing, without a bra on. It's strange, but refreshing. Well, then again, it wasn't refreshing to get another rash from using acne cream on one tiny pimple (top of the chest), nor was it refreshing to feel a little "rock" at the bottom of rightie as I sat down to type. Oh well. Boobs are weird.

June 23, 2014:

Long time, no write? Ooopsie. But, kids, I have an excuse! I was in Canada, of all places, from June 8-14. And then last week was another clusterfuck of crazy activities smacked together into a week. Oooofta.

Let me sum up:

The Chair Academy was in Canmore, Alberta, Canada. I think I used up my allotted amount of f-bombs that first travel day – sorry, Gma! – but once we got to Canmore, and the Canadian Rockies were RIGHT FREAKING THERE, I felt like I might have found my favorite place on earth.

I traveled to this week-long conference with two buddies from campus who are also in the campus' Leadership Academy (with me). They kept me calm. They made me laugh. They understood my anger and small bits of cynicism about the conference.

In addition to them, I also feel like the mountains & the people of Canmore showed me what contentment looks like. That town – kind of like the poor man's Banff – is full of active people. Many people were hiking, walking, running, and biking on any given day. That is my kind of vibe!

The air was different, too. I did stay active while we were there with a few early morning runs and bike rides (the resort had free rentals!) if only to say "Hi" to the Three Sisters Mountains & to be able to eat the sugar-based snacks at break time (seriously, they weren't really ideal; people need protein!).

I had a few epiphanies about myself. First of all, one of the surveys we took pre-conference listed "Intellection" as one of my strengths. This means I like to think a lot. A LOT A LOT. So, it makes sense that when I bring an idea to a committee or meeting, and they crap on it, my first reaction is to get mad. BUT that's because they don't know how long I've been thinking about that idea. They might think I'm tossing it in there for shits and giggles. And I'm not. I am also "Strategic" as another strength, which means I find the best route to make the idea WORK. Yeah. And to add to all that, I also have "Input" as a strength, and that means I collect ideas all the damn time. No WONDER I am exhausted. For real.

The second epiphany that I told Jan about almost the minute I got home was that it has always bugged me – in a positive way – as to why he & I have been together so long when we look at the world SO differently. We are politically polar opposites, we buy things in different ways and he gets buyer's remorse a lot, my family connections are very different than his, etc. But if he were to take this survey, I think he'd be built on the inside like I am. We think a lot. This fence project – and many of our home improvement projects – have not seen a lot of fights from us because we've had similar thoughts about what to do & what will work best. We are both inputting and intellecting and strategerizing very similarly. Does that make sense?

Yeah.

My last tiny epiphany was when one of the facilitator's didn't seem to "get me." I just didn't like him. And it occurred to me that I'm okay when people don't like me, yet I ponder and ponder why I don't like someone else. Well, maybe I just don't, and that's the end of the story.

Cut to getting home and my dad's parents are in town before they go on an adventure to see the farm out west and all the oil chaos. A few of us ladies decide to go downtown to a little vintage shop, and I show my Gma (and sister-in-law who loves owls) this chubby little owl sculpture. I say, "I wonder why I like these chubby things so much," and my Gma says, "Maybe because you were chubby, and now you're not." Huh. Good call, Gma. Good call.

I really wish that weekend would've been longer because it was nice to see everyone (due to it being Father's Day, my siblings all came to town either Saturday or Sunday), and I could've gotten more rest before driving my tired soul to Valley City for an Englishly teacherly taskforce conference thingie (doesn't that description allude to so much?). I definitely needed more time between that and The Chair Academy. I was almost bummed and felt a little lost after being in Canada. To go from that experience to an unfocused taskforce meeting was detrimental to my "buzz." It's like I lost my intellectual boner.

We couldn't really figure out what we were doing there, but at least we were all together using our creative brains. I was, and still am, concerned that no one used the awesome handout we came up with as a group LAST summer. I mean, if you want to pay me to create something every summer and then not use it, okay... but isn't that just wasted money? Eh, maybe I shouldn't care. Okay, I don't. I do love that when a few of us did dinner on Tuesday night, we all shared teaching ideas. God, I love networking over a cocktail!

On the way home Wednesday (June 18), I stopped in Fargo to get the bug's oil changed and, of course, hit my favorite shops. At Savers, I scored a beautiful navy nightgown (with triangles of lace for the boobage area) and a few wireless bras that I would have NEVER been able to pull off pre-surgery. I already wore one under a tank that had small straps.

Before my surgery, I wouldn't have worn those damn tanks... well, I also thought my upper arms were too large as well (still working on that assessment as I type).

June 25, 2014:

After one too many drinks last night at sand volleyball, I left my sports bra on (and didn't even brush my teeth either!) and zonked out. So, of course, this morning I would wake up to a pimple on the under side of leftie. And when I saw it, I almost thought it was something worse, for about five seconds. But then, like, what could it have been? A tiny pink tumor with a white top out to take down my boobie empire? My brain goes from zero to sixty too quickly, I tell ya.

So, I popped it and put on just a tank top. The end.

June 27, 2014:

Here are a few things I know for certain:
--- My right armpit stinks more than my left.
--- My breath isn't always the greatest.
--- You can change your thoughts; a year ago, I would've craved a brownie in the afternoon... now, I'm like, "Chop up that big juicy apple & throw some cinnamon on it. Oh yeah, that's the ticket."

Chapter 24: Conclusion.

Since I know it's going to be UBER difficult for me to conclude... I'll take something from Sloane Crosley's book, <u>How Did You Get This Number</u>:

"There is one thing you know for sure, one fact that never fails to comfort you: the worst day of your life wasn't in there, in that mess. And it will do you good to remember that the best day of your life wasn't in there, either. But another person* brought you closer to those borders than you had been, and maybe that's not such a bad thing."

(*And that person could be YOU. Or me. Yeah, whatever.)

And this too: "Somewhere in the center of all that bargaining and investing and stealing is meaning and truth and the lessons you have always known. You hope so. Because without meaning, it was all just a bunch of someone else's stuff" (271).

"There are fulcrum moments in life when you can feel your world pivot in a new direction. Everything that mattered doesn't. There is no adjustment period between the old and the new" (63). I don't think Sloane was talking about just her body with these sentences, but I connect to that with their meanings. I'm on a new road. This road might include more spaghetti straps and braless adventures, it might include more weight-lifting (reading & trying out the program in <u>The New Rules of Lifting for Women: Lift Like a Man, Look Like a Goddess</u>), and it most definitely will include more confidence.

Triple B, baby. Yeppers. B to the third power... and those three powers are the trifecta of being smart, funny, and independent!

BBB

References.

Crosley, Sloane. <u>How Did You Get This Number</u>. New York:
    Riverhead Books, 2010.
Sandler, Lauren. "None is Enough." <u>TIME</u>. 12 August 13. Pgs 38-45.

BBB

Attributions.

Cover image of one of my besties Fran & I at her wedding in 2005.

Appendix (Chapter 25).

Me:
I want to see you before your surgery, if possible.

KJ:
Oh sweetie, me too!!! It got pushed back to the 10th. Doctor conflict. BUT much to chat about! [...] How about Tuesday lunch? I could still have a beverage & I can hear about your recent adventures, I can talk about the new freedom without Carrie and you can further inspire me with your awesome chest! Wear something low cut!!!

Me:
YES TUESDAY LUNCH! I would love to see you this weekend, BUT Emmett (and his parents blahblahblah) is swimming out at their place Friday, and I get to join him. He's a little water bug!
[...] Wow. Yes, we have to catch up. We should invite the other ladies, and I'll try to come to lunch braless as inspiration!

Me:
I'm using you as a reason to wrap up the BBB; I'm sure you knew that. I also think you should read <u>The New Rules of Lifting for Women</u> as you recover = it's more about eating mini-meals, more protein, and lifting weights 3x a week to make a lean, mean body. I'm trying the first workout tonight.

KJ:
You are such a - well, inspiration, rock, release... I don't know what word to use, but I am not an Englisher (not in my phone dictionary) and maybe there isn't one word to describe how special you are and what you mean to me. Yes, I am crying. (Can I use dot dot dot there?).

Me:
Oh sweetie! Big hug from the locker room. I'm sweating tears for ya. Just THINK, in a year, you'll be sending me baby boobie pics!

So much "weight" will be lifted in a little over a week! I know you'll have a different recovery than I did, but I plan to jet out to see you WHENEVER you need me.

KJ:
Thanks so much!

About the Author.

Sybil Priebe lives in Wahpeton, ND, with her boyfriend and bitchy cat. She teaches at a community & technical college in southeastern North Dakota. In her spare time, she likes to write, read unconventional literature, work on remodeling projects, drive her VW bug, shop at secondhand stores, do some crafting, go on bike rides, and occasionally run 5Ks and half marathons.

Contact her at: ihaveabug@yahoo.com

www.ingramcontent.com/pod-product-compliance
Lightning Source LLC
Chambersburg PA
CBHW071524040426
42452CB00008B/876